Hercules—The Panto!!

A pantomime

Julia Banks

Samuel French — London
New York - Toronto - Hollywood

© 1999 BY SAMUEL FRENCH LTD

Rights of Performance by Amateurs are controlled by Samuel French Ltd, 52 Fitzroy Street, London W1P 6JR, and they, or their authorized agents, issue licences to amateurs on payment of a fee. **It is an infringement of the Copyright to give any performance or public reading of the play before the fee has been paid and the licence issued.**

The Royalty Fee indicated below is subject to contract and subject to variation at the sole discretion of Samuel French Ltd.

>   Basic fee for each and every
>   performance by amateurs   Code L
>   in the British Isles

The publication of this play does not imply that it is necessarily available for performance by amateurs or professionals, either in the British Isles or Overseas. Amateurs and professionals considering a production are strongly advised in their own interests to apply to the appropriate agents for consent before starting rehearsals or booking a theatre or hall.

ISBN 0 573 16440 1

Please see page iv for further copyright information

LINCOLNSHIRE
COUNTY COUNCIL

822

HERCULES—THE PANTO!!

First presented by the Mana Little Theatre in The Studio, Plimmerton, New Zealand on 22nd July 1998, with the following cast:

Wanda	Abby Govier
Hercules	Grant Roa
Narcissus	Tim Barlow
Venus	Nicola Brough
Medusa	Tony Tait
Griffin	Michael Wesley-Smith
The King	Cliff Thomas
Knit	Dorothy-Anne Bonner
Purl	Cheryll Shoesmith
Drop One	Pamela Lockwood
Zoë	Nicola Brough
Chloë	Lizzie Wesley-Smith

With Megan Doile, Judy Jeffery, Sophie Ward, Margie Faber, Harriet Laws, Ashton Henty, Noël Dowrick, Warrick Proctor, John Wilce

Directed by **Maureen Aitken**

COPYRIGHT INFORMATION

(See also page ii)

This play is fully protected under the Copyright Laws of the British Commonwealth of Nations, the United States of America and all countries of the Berne and Universal Copyright Conventions.

All rights including Stage, Motion Picture, Radio, Television, Public Reading, and Translation into Foreign Languages, are strictly reserved.

No part of this publication may lawfully be reproduced in ANY form or by any means — photocopying, typescript, recording (including video-recording), manuscript, electronic, mechanical, or otherwise—or be transmitted or stored in a retrieval system, without prior permission.

Licences for amateur performances are issued subject to the understanding that it shall be made clear in all advertising matter that the audience will witness an amateur performance; that the names of the authors of the plays shall be included on all programmes; and that the integrity of the authors' work will be preserved.

The Royalty Fee is subject to contract and subject to variation at the sole discretion of Samuel French Ltd.

In Theatres or Halls seating Four Hundred or more the fee will be subject to negotiation.

In Territories Overseas the fee quoted above may not apply. A fee will be quoted on application to our local authorized agent, or if there is no such agent, on application to Samuel French Ltd, London.

VIDEO-RECORDING OF AMATEUR PRODUCTIONS

Please note that the copyright laws governing video-recording are extremely complex and that it should not be assumed that any play may be video-recorded for whatever purpose without first obtaining the permission of the appropriate agents. The fact that a play is published by Samuel French Ltd does not indicate that video rights are available or that Samuel French Ltd controls such rights.

Subsequently presented by the Howick Operatic Society at the Harlequin Theatre, Howick, Auckland, New Zealand, on 21st November 1998, with the following cast:

Wanda	Penne Clayton
Hercules	Geofferson Wilsher
Narcissus	David Scordino
Venus	Julie Moore
Medusa	Rex McIntosh
Griffin	Domini Calder
The King	Paul Diver
Knit	Lisa Hewlett
Purl	Kristie Gailey
Drop One	Kristina Mason
Zoë	Katherine Bolt
Chloë	Lesley Hodder

Directed by the author—**Julia Banks**

MUSICAL NUMBERS

The choice of songs and dance music is left to the individual director although the author has provided a list of song suggestions which is available upon request. Not all of the numbers listed here and in the script need be included. Permission from Samuel French Ltd to perform HERCULES—THE PANTO!! does not include permission to use any copyright songs or music within the pantomime. Please read the note supplied by the Performing Right Society (on page viii) very carefully.

ACT I

1. Venus
2. Wanda and Greek Chorus
3. Male Chorus
4. Hercules and Narcissus
5. The Three Fates
6. Narcissus and Hercules
7. Medusa and Narcissus
8. Rap by Leader of the Red Guards
9. The King
10. Hercules
11. Hercules, Narcissus, Medusa, King, Greek Chorus, Cheerleaders and Bodyguards

ACT II

12. Medusa
13. Instrumental
    Reprise of No 7
    Reprise of No 7 (madcap speed)
    Reprise of No 13
14. The Three Fates
15. Hercules and Narcissus
16. Venus
17. Wanda (and Hercules)

18	The Three Fates
	Music—dance
19	Demons' song and dance
20	Reprise of Song 16—Hercules and Wanda
21	Wanda
22	King, backed by Chorus
23	Hercules and Cast

The notice printed below on behalf of the Performing Right Society should be carefully read if any copyright music is used in this play.

The permission of the owner of the performing rights in copyright music must be obtained before any public performance may be given, whether in conjunction with a play or sketch or otherwise, and this permission is just as necessary for amateur performances as for professional. The majority of copyright musical works (other than oratorios, musical plays and similar dramatico-musical works) are controlled in the British Commonwealth by the PERFORMING RIGHT SOCIETY LTD, 29-33 Berners Street, London W1P 4AA.

The Society's practice is to issue licences authorizing the use of its repertoire to the proprietors of premises at which music is publicly performed, or, alternatively, to the organizers of musical entertainments, but the Society does not require payment of fees by performers as such. Producers or promoters of plays, sketches, etc., at which music is to be performed, during or after the play or sketch, should ascertain whether the premises at which their performances are to be given are covered by a licence issued by the Society, and if they are not, should make application to the Society for particulars as to the fee payable.

A separate and additional licence from PHONOGRAPHIC PERFORMANCES LTD, 1 Upper James Street, London W1R 3HG, is needed whenever commercial recordings are used.

CHARACTERS

Venus, goddess of love (2 people)
Gryphon
Princess Wanda
Hercules
Narcissus
The King
Knit
Purl   The Three Fates
Drop One
Medusa
Cyclops, the villain (played by 2 people)
Chloë
Zoë   Princess's handmaids
Guard Leader
Slaves
Greek Chorus
Nymphs
Cheerleaders
Demons
Guards

SYNOPSIS OF SCENES

ACT I

SCENE 1   Frontcloth: The Greek Chorus

SCENE 2   The Mountain Top

SCENE 3   The Palace. Princess Wanda's TV Room

SCENE 4   The YMCA

SCENE 5   Frontcloth: The Three Fates

SCENE 6   The Royal Heir Beauty Salon

SCENE 7   Frontcloth: The Red Guards

SCENE 8   The Palace

ACT II

SCENE 1   The Royal Heir Beauty Salon

SCENE 2   Frontcloth: Medusa's Cleanup

SCENE 3   The River Styx

SCENE 4   The Mountain Top

SCENE 5   Frontcloth: Hercules and Wanda

SCENE 6   Cyclop's Grotto

SCENE 7   Frontcloth: Earthquake

SCENE 8   The Palace

AUTHOR'S NOTE

Hercules—the Panto!! is an all-new look at a very popular character. I began writing this pantomine at the beginning of 1997, little knowing that a film (which I have not seen) also featuring our hero was heading this way. My epic probably bears little resemblance to that or any other version—I hope! Despite its fresh topic, *Hercules—the Panto!!* is a traditional-style pantomime, written on two levels to appeal to adults and children at the same time.

Songs (which are suggestions only) may be replaced, added or omitted if desired.

Some local shop names etc. will need to be inserted, and some references—especially to political and show business personalities—may need to be altered to suit the time and place.

I hope you enjoy *Hercules—The Panto!!* That's what it's there for!

Julia Banks

CAST DESCRIPTION

Greek Chorus About six to eight women, any age, who chant the verses that tell the story and literally set the scene. They also sing some choruses. Although a very formal group at first, they loosen up during the story's unfolding.

Venus She is the Goddess of Love; mysterious, glamorous and powerful, who arranges for Hercules to find his True Love. Venus stays in one place, on the mountain top, and has four arms which she moves independently. She is, of course, composed of two women. Although she uses a microphone, Venus must have a powerful singing style.

Gryphon This mythological creature can be played by a male or female but he calls himself a male. He is lovable, bouncy and a little bumbly. His body is covered with gingery fur so Wanda gives him the name "Gingernut". Although he has an eagle's head he must appear gentle and shy. Gingernut, who may be played by an actor of any age, must establish a good rapport with the audience. This is a non-singing, non-dancing character.

Wanda The Princess. She is bossy, self-centred, vain, self-indulgent and arrogant, with a very low opinion of everyone, especially men. She will become a much nicer person as her relationship with her first and only friend, the Gryphon, develops. She is young, attractive, and must be able to sing. At the end she will have become a woman worthy of our hero, Hercules.

Hercules The man himself! He must be of good stature, as attractively well-built as possible and reasonably young. He will be All Male. This part must be played straight, with great intensity and commitment. Hercules is aware that he is the strongest man in the world but he is still modest. He has an American accent, and must be able to sing.

Narcissus He has been Hercules' sidekick during the Twelve Labours, and he also has as American accent. Young, fun-loving and mischievous, he is going to work with his Auntie who has just opened "The Royal Heir Beauty Salon". Being very vain, he expects to be quite happy there amongst the mirrors. This role preferably requires ability as a dancer, comedian and singer.

The King Elvis of course … who else!? This is a singing, rocking part portraying "The King" in his later, fuller-figured years; the white rhinestoned jumpsuit era. He has a slow Southern drawl. His great fear is that his daughter will marry Michael Jackson!

The Fates They are Knit, Purl and Drop One (the last is rather addle-brained). These are three women packed with sexy pizzazz! They can be any age as long as they are full of life and personality. The Three Fates are constantly spinning (the Wheel of Fortune) and knitting the Lives of us mere mortals. To us they appear to have a very cavalier attitude towards this important task. They must be able to sing in three-part harmony, dance and knit!

Medusa A playful, ageing vamp with an upper-class English "plum in her mouth", (which she sometimes forgets, lapsing into a rather "common" tone). Medusa is the traditional dame and must be played to the hilt. This is a fun role for a male comedian, the bigger and taller the better! Medusa is looking for a mate but, having snakes instead of hair, she has a limited appeal. This role demands a lot of slapstick, plus some singing.

Cyclops The Villain. He is only seen in the second act and is actually a huge puppet. He remains seated on his great throne throughout. Cyclop's operator (Cyc One) stands inside the figure to manipulate it. Cyclop's deep, reverberating voice comes from another offstage actor (Cyc Two), whose microphone has speakers near Cyclop's head. Cyclops consists of two non-singing and (obviously!) non-dancing roles.

Chloë & Zoë Speaking parts as servants. They may also double up in the Chorus etc.

Nymphs Female dancers accompanying the Goddess on the mountaintop. They include three small speaking parts.

Cheerleaders 8 appealing girl dancers in minikilts, waving pompoms.

Demons Male and/or female dancers—can be the Cheerleaders/Nymphs.

Guards Male chorus. If they are also dancers, all the better. However, the kung fu movements could, if desired, be performed by youngsters with kung fu ability while the male chorus simply strikes poses.

Leader Male Leader of the Red Guards with a small speaking part and one song.

NB: Nymphs, Demons, Cheerleaders, Slaves, Red Guards and Bodyguards can all be the same company members. If children are to be included in the cast, they can be Demons, Nymphs etc.

ACT I

Scene 1

Frontcloth

Against the backdrop of black curtains the Greek Chorus enters L. They solemnly take their places, hands clasped before them, and intone

Chorus Once, long ago when Time was young
And all the stars were newly-hung
When thunder rolled from dusk to dawn
And mountains were but moments born,
'Twas then each god and goddess fair
On pretty sandalled feet went here.

Or flew upon the zephyr breeze...
To whither he or she did please.
And far below their lofty portals
Dwelt the folk like us, mere mortals
Living lives of joy ... or boredom
As The Fates decided for them.

Of gods too numerous to mention
One deserves our full attention.
Others were both good and bold,
But still, from all those tales of old
Greatest of the lot of these,
Was brave and mighty—*Hercules*!

Eight Cheerleaders burst on stage, four from each side, to spell out the name of "Hercules". They perform typical cheerleader movements

One (*shouting*) Give us an "H"!
Two (*shouting*) Give us an "E"!
Three (*shouting*) Give us an "R"!
Four (*shouting*) Give us a "C"!
Five (*shouting*) Give us a "U"!

Six (*shouting*) "L"!
Seven (*shouting*) "E"!
Eight (*shouting*) "S"!
All (*shouting*) HERCULES!!

They stay lined up across C *and repeat this chant and movements, jumping excitedly into the air on the last word. The Chorus is most annoyed*

Chorus   What is this frightful fuss about?
How *dare* you yell? How *dare* you shout?
We simply *won't* be superceded!
Begone with you until you're needed.

The Chorus points imperiously to the exit L

   Cheerleaders exit rather sulkily

The Chorus composes itself and continues

Chorus   Yes, brave young Hercules, our hero
Knew no boundaries ... knew no fear, oh
Naught could keep him from his duty!
None could match his peerless beauty!
Now returning to his neighbours
After doing Twelve Hard Labours
Who should watch him from above
But Venus... Goddess of True Love

Scene 2

The mountain top

There is a very dramatic crack of thunder, lightning, purple spot, dry ice

Song 1 (Venus)

The CURTAINS *part to reveal full-stage scene of the goddess on the mountain top. This is a big, powerful production number*

   On the second verse the Nymphs enter from both sides, singing and dancing. The Chorus enters L *at the same time as the Nymphs, and stands* L, *while also singing the choruses*

Act I, Scene 2   3

At the end of the number the Nymphs sink around the mountain and lie in graceful langour

Venus (*majestically*) I am Venus, the Goddess of Love! All who have ever loved, have loved through me. But there is one who has never yet tasted such joys! Brave Hercules, returning from far-off lands, has performed his Labours well, but for little reward. I think it is time young Hercules found—True Love!
Nymph 1 (*leaping up*) Oh mistress, let *me* be the Love of Hercules!
Nymph 2 (*leaping up*) No, let *me*, oh mistress!
Nymph 3 (*leaping up*) Please, mistress... *me*! ME!

All the Nymphs are now on their feet and eagerly begging the goddess in great excitement

As Venus speaks, her "back" hands take out a large volume which was concealed in the mountain top. It bears the bold title: "This is Your Wife"

Venus (*dramatically*) SILENCE! The True Love of Hercules has already been chosen. I have had her on my books for some time. Ah, here it is! (*She points to the page*) Hercules's True Love will be the only child of the King—the beautiful Princess Wanda.
Nymph 1 (*in horror*) Princess *Wanda*!?
Nymph 2 (*in disbelief*) Not *the* Princess Wanda!?
Nymph 3 (*in despair*) The nastiest girl in the Kingdom!?
Venus The same!
Nymph 1 How could anyone love *her*!
Nymph 2 Especially someone like *Hercules*!
Nymph 3 The bravest, strongest...
All Nymphs (*almost swooning*) ...Handsomest man in the Kingdom!!
Venus Silence, Nymphs! I have made my decision. And that is that! (*She slams the book shut, nearly catching a third hand in it, in a moment of uncoordination*)
Nymph 1 (*spitting out the name*) Wanda! Huh! How could Hercules love anyone named after a *fish*!
Venus (*sternly*) I said that is *enough*! Hercules will find his love at last... Yes... (*Musingly*) The Thirteenth Labour of Hercules! It could prove the most difficult of them all...

She breaks off, noticing and pointing R to a creature lurking shyly in the wings, watching her—it is the Gryphon

(*Imperiously*) And what have we here?

Two Nymphs go over and bring the Gryphon C, *to face the goddess, head bowed. He is quivering with fright*

Well?
Gryphon (*looking up and up until at last he sees her face*) Oh, your very very high highness... I... I've come to b-beg a b-boon.
Venus "Beg a baboon"!?

Pause

You want me to give you a *monkey*!?
Gryphon No, your very great greatness. I m-mean I want to *beg* a *boon*.
Venus Oh! How quaint! And *what* "boon" exactly do you want to "beg"?
Gryphon Please, your lofty loftiness... I... I ... want t-to be able to fly.
Venus (*dismissively*) Well, my dear, *everyone* wants to fly. *You* should be all right, though. What are those things on your back? (*She points at him with all four arms, one after the other*) Back-scratchers!? (*Smiling at her own wit, she looks around for approval*)

Nymphs titter obligingly

Gryphon They're wings, All-Seeing One.
Venus (*blithely*) Then use them. (*She looks at his downcast face*)

Pause

Have you got a problem with that?
Gryphon Well ... they don't work. That's why I've c-come to *you*. (*Boldly, to the audience*) I thought that Venus, the Goddess of Love, could do *any*thing.
Venus Well yes, of course I can! On the other hand... (*She does some business waving her arms trying to decide which is the "other" hand*) What can you do for *me* in exchange?
Gryphon Um. Well... You see, I'm a gryphon. (*Blurting it out*) But I don't actually know what gryphons are *for*...!? (*His voice trails off*) If you see what I mean... (*He bows his head miserably*)
Venus Hmm. I didn't realize "gryphons"actually existed. I've always thought you were simply a *mythological* beast. Let me see now—what could you do? (*After a pause she is struck by an idea*) I know! A Friend! Could you be Friend, do you think?
Gryphon Um, yes, I suppose so. Ah, whose Friend. (*Anxiously*) Yours?
Venus The gods forbid! No, I'm thinking of someone who will need to change her ways before she can find Love. Perhaps having a Friend will be the first step. Yes! You must become the Friend of—Princess Wanda.

Act I, Scene 3   5

Gryphon (*horrifed*) Princess *Wanda!* Not *the* Princess Wanda! The nastiest girl in the Kingdom!
Venus (*to the audience*) Haven't we been down this road before? (*To the Gryphon*) That's the deal. You befriend Princess Wanda and I'll give you the power to fly. Take it or leave it.
Gryphon I'll take it! (*To himself*) Wanda can't be as bad as all that ... she *can't* be! Nobody can ... can they...?

Gryphon exits R, *muttering*

CURTAINS *close on this scene and the Chorus exits* L

We hear the final strains of a TV theme

SCENE 3

The Palace. The Princess's TV room

This scene takes place in front of a mid-stage traveller

Chloë enters L *and deposits a small table holding a glass of wine, a packet of gingernut biscuits, a plate of fruit and an archaic conchshell "telephone"*

The Princess is pushed on by Chorus members. She is reclining on a chaise longue and watching a portable TV set wheeled on in front of her by Zoë

The Chorus exits L

The music ends and the Princess brandishes a remote control to "change TV channels"

Wanda (*cattily mimicking the sales pitch of the commercial*) "Nutural Glow for thut reelly nutural look." Boring, boring, boring... (*She changes channels with the remote control and mimicks again*) "Only at Michael Hill—Jooller". Boring! (*She "turns off" the TV with the remote control. Imperiously, to her servants*) Bring me a grape.
Chloë (*coming forward with a plate of fruit*) Here you are, Princess Wanda.
Wanda (*picking up a grape, she makes a face and almost spits the words in Chloë's face*) Peel it!

Zoë comes forward with a potato peeler. She tries clumsily to peel the grape with it

6 Hercules—The Panto!!

Zoë Oops!
Wanda You ham-fisted ox! Look what you've done! I shall report you to Daddy. What is your name?
Zoë Zoë, your Highness.
Wanda And you?
Chloë Chloë, your Highness.
Wanda How long have you been my maidservants?
Zoë }
Chloë } (*together; very deliberately*) Fifteen years, your Highness.
Wanda Hmm. I thought you looked familiar. (*On the attack again*) Well, you're useless, the pair of you. I can't think why Daddy employed you in the first place.
Zoë (*very matter-of-factly*) Because no-one else answered his advertisements, Princess Wanda.
Chloë The King put "Help Wanted" ads in… (*she counts them off one by one on her fingers*) the *Telegraph*, the *Observer*, *The Guardian*, *The Times*…
Zoë (*taking over and also counting them off*) The *Independent*, the *Sun*, the *Mirror*, *News of the World*…
Wanda (*cutting in*) Yeah, yeah, yeah. Anyway; you're still fired! (*Airily*) You'll just have to advertise again.
Chloë We *have* been advertising again, your Highness.
Wanda For how long?
Zoë Fifteen years, your Highness. We've advertised on Radio 1, Radio 2, Radio 3, Scottish Radio, Virgin Radio… (*She counts off again*)
Chloë (*continuing counting off*) Kiss FM, ITV, BBC 1, BBC 2…
Wanda (*quickly*) OK, OK! Fine. Well, I won't sack you *this* time.
Chloë }
Zoë } (*together; resignedly*) Thank you, your Highness.
Wanda (*muttering*) Don't say I'm not good to you…

The phone rings. It should toll like a handbell

Chloë (*answering it in a bored sing-song recital*) Hullo-oh! The-Royal-Palace-Princess-Wanda's-TV-Room-we-hope-you're-having-a-happy-day-Chloë-speaking-how-may-I-help-you. (*She pauses then speaks very sharply*) Yep. She's here. (*She hands the phone to Wanda*) It's for you.
Wanda (*oozing charm*) Hullo!? (*She listens then rolls her eyes heavenward. After a longish pause*) I don't care if you *do* think I'm beautiful. I'm not going to marry you. (*After a longish pause*) I don't care if your mother *does* think we'd make a good match. I'm still not going to marry you. (*She pauses. Angrily*) I don't care if you *are* going to be the King of England, Charles … the answer's still *no*!! (*She slams down the receiver*)

Act I, Scene 3   7

> Song 2 (Wanda and Greek Chorus)
>
> *During this song Zoë and Chloë exit L and return for the second verse, leading the Chorus across in a protest march. They are all holding up placards with funny feminist slogans (see Production Notes for suggestions)*
>
> *After the song, the Chorus, Chloë and Zoë move to exit L. As they do so, the Gryphon sidles on L in front of them. They stop and remark*

Chorus   But lo! Who comest wand'ring here
               It is the Gryphon, I declare!
               He's either very brave or foolish
               To take as "Friend" a girl so mulish.

Chorus exit L

Gryphon *(shyly)* Er, hullo. Are you Wanda? S-sorry, um, *Princess* Wanda? I couldn't find anyone so I thought I'd better just make my… *(He falters)* Own way. Here. To you…
Wanda *(gaping)* Oh my giddy aunt! *(She points rudely to the Gryphon, asking the audience)* What on earth is that! A walking hearth-rug!?
Gryphon *(bravely)* I'm a gryphon.
Wanda A gryphon! *(Derisively)* You've got to be kidding! *(She pauses)* So what are gryphons *for*?
Gryphon Well, I hope they might be for… Friends?
Wanda *(stroppily)* Friends? Friends? Whose Friend?
Gryphon *(with a big breath—it's now or never)* Y-yours.
Wanda *(proudly)* I've never had a friend in my life, and I don't intend to start now.
Gryphon *(brightening—they have something in common)* Neither have I. I think it'd be fun. *(He chummily sits beside her)*

Wanda gives him such a thunderous look, he jumps up smartly

Wanda Fun! *(She sneers)* How could a Friend be fun?
Gryphon Well, I suppose we could do things together. Go places … see things…
Wanda Huh. *(She thinks about it)* So what's your name?
Gryphon I don't seem to have one…
Wanda Then I'll give you a name! Kneel!
Gryphon *(brightly)* Neil!? Thanks! That's a nice name!
Wanda Silly. Kneel down. *(She waves the packet of gingernut biscuits in the air)* Just look at the colour of you—you're definitely ginger—just like my

favourite bickies! (*She dubs him on the shoulder with the biscuit packet*) I officially name you—Gingernut. Gryphon Gingernut!
Gryphon Gingernut!? Great! Do I call you Wanda?
Wanda You certainly do not. It's *Princess* Wanda to you. That's if I let you talk to me at all. (*She pauses*) So, what exactly *is* a gryphon?
Gryphon I believe I'm what's known as a "mythological beast".
Wanda (*haughtily*) Oh, so you're a *myth*, are you?
Gryphon (*defensively, head high*) I thertainly am not! I'm a *mithter*.
Wanda (*laughing*) Well, maybe I will let you stay. At least you're more fun than that dreary old pile of crumpled bedlinen... (*She flaps her hand scornfully towards* L *to indicate where the Chorus exited earlier*) Now buzz off, Gingernut! I've got an appointment at the new Beauty Salon in a couple of hours and I've got my weightlifting workout first.
Gryphon (*impressed*) Gosh! Weightlifting!
Wanda (*smugly*) Oh, that's nothing! Today I've also got Step Aerobics, Body Sculpting and Muscle Building. (*She "turns on" the TV*)
Gryphon (*overawed*) Gee, you're gonna be tired!
Wanda Not really. (*She yawns*) I usually lie down to watch...

Chorus members enter L *and wheel out Wanda as she lies back watching the TV. Zoë and Chloë clear the table and TV. All exit* L, *except the Gryphon*

The tabs close behind the Gryphon as he moves forward to talk to the audience

Gryphon That went really well, don't you think? Hullo! Is there anybody out there? Hullo! (*He cups his "ear" to listen for a reply*) Do you know who I am? I've got a name now, just like you! Do you remember it? Yes, Gingernut! I'm Gryphon Gingernut! Hullo everybody. Say, "Hullo, Gingernut"! (*Try this out with lots of encouragement*) I'm so happy. Do you know why? Because I've got a Friend. Hands up if *you've* got a friend! (*He puts his hand up too*) Maybe we can *all* be friends. Well, I'm off to measure my wings. Do you think they've grown any bigger yet? See you soon! Bye everyone! (*He gets the audience to call "Goodbye Gingernut"*)

Gryphon exits R *waving to the audience*

Act I, Scene 4

Scene 4

The YMCA

Song 3 (Male Chorus)

The CURTAINS *part to reveal the full stage. A sign tells us this is the YMCA. The male chorus are involved in some impressive exercise routines and striking up muscleman poses. They perform a vigorous dance and encourage the audience to sing along and to shout out the chorus*

After this number they range around the sides as the Cheerleaders suddenly bounce in from each side US. *They end up in a line across the front that spells—"Hercules"*

One Give us an "H"!
Two Give us an "E"!
Three Give us an "R"!
Four Give us a "C"!
Five Give us a "U"!
Six "L"!
Seven "E"!
Eight "S"!
All HERCULES!!... (*They leap in the air*)

This procedure is repeated while the men appreciatively look on from the sides

Hercules enters US

He strolls down the aisle made by the men and the Cheerleaders who part to stand four on each side. The Cheerleaders go through their routine once more, getting the audience to call out the letters with them—as each of the girls steps forward, she—and they—will call out the letter on her T-shirt to spell out "Hercules". Hercules steps forward C, *strikes a muscleman pose and holds it, awaiting recognition*

Hercules Thanks! Thanks everyone! Gee, I gotta tell ya, those Twelve Labours were pretty tough. Especially cleaning out the Aegean Stables! Whew, the work just kept piling up! (*He indicates it "piling up" with his hands*) But I've washed my hands of that now. (*Aside*) Let me tell ya; I needed to! Hey, guess what else I cleaned up last night? The Mr Knotty Ash Contest!
Cheerleaders Mr Knotty Ash! Hercules *won*!! Yay, *Hercules*!

They leap and wave their pompoms. When they regroup they are in a different line and their T-shirts spell out "CHEERS". Those with "U" and "L" simply stand aside and point it out

Hercules (*modestly*) Yep, I won. So now I'm off to the Biggie ... Mr Universe.
Cheerleaders You'll win! Mr Universe! Yay, *Hercules*! (*They leap some more. This time their T-shirts spell "HE RULES"*)
Hercules (*looking round*) Hey, any of you guys seen Narcissus?

Narcissus enters US

Narcissus Yo! Over here, Herc!
Hercules Yo, Narcissus! Gimme five!

They exchange a high five which leaves Narcissus blowing on his hand to ease the pain

Hey, glad I caught ya, Narc! I'm outta here! (*He strikes a pose*) Mr Universe Contest, here I come!

Narcissus gives a playful punch on Hercules's shoulder. It nearly breaks his hand

Narcissus You'll win it, Herc, no problem.
Hercules (*humbly*) Aw, ya think so?

He returns the playful punch which floors his friend. Hercules helps him up and brushes him

Cheerleaders (*chanting*) You'll win! You'll win! You'll win, *Hercules*! (*They repeat this chant, with pompom waving and highkicks*)
Hercules (*embarrassed*) Aw ... hey, I gotta tell ya, it's been great hangin' out with you guys. But a he-man's gotta do what a he-man's gotta do. (*He shakes hands with some of the men, says goodbye, and slaps them on the back*)

They over-react to show up his strength

Men exit UL

Cheerleaders hug Hercules then follow the men off, calling back loving "goodbyes" to Hercules

Act I, Scene 5   11

Narcissus Gee, Herc, I can't wait to settle down again. I'm lookin' to a nice quiet life.
Hercules So what'll ya do, Narc?
Narcissus Well, I'm gonna help my Auntie with this great little business she's just set up. I'll be living on Easy Street!
Hercules So it's some kinda shop, is it, Narc?
Narcissus Well, it's not exactly a *shop*, Herc. It's ... uh ... well ... a beauty salon.
Hercules A BEAUTY SALON!?
Narcissus (*defensively*) Yeah; a Beauty Salon! I happen to think that personal appearance is real important.
Hercules (*grinning*) Yeah, Narcissus. You're the only guy I know who's got a mirror on his bathroom ceiling so he can watch himself gargle...
Narcissus (*smoothing his hair*) What are ya saying, Herc? Do ya think I'm vain or somethin'?
Hercules Now why would ya say that?
Narcissus Oh, it's just that people as good-looking as me usually are.
Hercules (*laughing*) So what's it called; this beauty salon?
Narcissus The Royal Heir—by Special Appointment to Her Royal Highness, Princess Wanda.
Hercules Not *the* Princess Wanda!? The... (*with the audience*) ...nastiest girl in the Kingdom!?
Narcissus That's the one! But my Auntie can handle her. *She's* got a Black Belt in karate and a Pink Purse in mugger-bashing!
Hercules So; a Beauty Salon, huh? Where *is* this setup?
Narcissus I told ya, Herc ... it's on Easy Street.
Hercules (*happily contemplating the future*) Ah... Easy Street...! Lead me to it!

Song 4 (Hercules and Narcissus)

They sing and dance a soft shoe shuffle, then exit UL

SCENE 5

Frontcloth

The Three Fates

The Chorus, divided into Demi-chorus and Semi-chorus, enter L

Chorus   Life is looking sweeter!

> Time to change the metre
> Of our little rhyme!
> Our hero's fame is growing;
> Soon he will be going
> To a foreign clime.
> And we know he's sure
> To scoop the pool once more
> With our collective blessing!
> While his friend Narcissus,
> With his Uncle's missis
> Soon will be hairdressing.

Demi-chorus (*looking at their watches*) Oops! We have to nip out,
> Take a little trip out—
> Time to change the scene;
> Introduce a threesome
> Who've turned out to be some
> *Very* funky team!

Demi-chorus exit L

The Semi-chorus gesture towards these departing Demi-chorus members with their thumbs

Semi-chorus They have gone to find
> Three ladies who are kind
> Of vital to the plot.
> Ladies who are knitting,
> Knitting without quitting
> Every chance they've got.
> Our lives are in their hand
> Each woman, child and man
> Our passions, loves and hates.
> To whom are we referring?
> None but the alluring
> Sisters—THE THREEEEEEE FATES!

The last three words are in the hyped-up style of an American TV games show commentator announcing the show's host. The Chorus members each point snappily towards the Three Fates' entrance with the forefinger of each hand

A vast trumpet fanfare

The Demi-chorus wheel on the Three Fates from L, *then exit* L. *The Three*

Act I, Scene 5   13

Fates are outrageous, colourful and sassy. As they are wheeled into view they are looking straight out at the audience, seated on three barstools all in a row. Behind them, on a pole, is a lottery wheel which is under a cover with "Wheel of Fortune" lettered on it. The three Fates are busy knitting lives. (See Production Notes)

The Demi-chorus exit L

Knit Hi! I'm Knit.
Purl I'm Purl.
Drop One I'm Drop One. (*She drops a stitch*) Ooops! (*She looks flustered*) Oh no! I just have!
All We're The Three Fates.
Knit (*bored*) All day long we sit here, spinning... (*She indicates the "Wheel of Fortune" behind*)
Purl (*bored*) And knitting...
Drop One (*bored*) And spinning...
Knit (*bored*) And knitting...
Purl (*fed up*) And spinning...
Drop One We knit *your* Life!
Knit And the way *we* knit it...
Purl ...is the way *you* live it.
Drop One (*smugly, she is a very childish character*) So there!
Knit (*pointing to someone in the audience*) We could be knitting *your* Life right now!
Purl (*pointing to another person*) Or yours!
Drop One (*to another*) Bet you hope *this* isn't yours! (*She giggles*)
Knit (*shaking her head*) It's a huge responsibility.
Purl (*nodding sagely*) And we take it very seriously.
Drop One (*fumbling*) Whoops! Made another mistake!
Knit Yet *another* mistake!?
Purl Whose life is it, anyway?
Drop One Jonathan Aitken's!
Knit (*shrugging*) Huh. What's one more mistake gonna matter...!?
Purl (*to the audience, pointing with her thumb at Drop One*) Guess who was knitting President Clinton last year! (*She winks*)
Drop One (*defensively*) I only dropped a few stitches...
Knit (*incredulously repeating her words*) Only dropped a few stitches!? You *unravelled* the poor guy!
Purl (*petulantly*) Oh, I feel like I've been knitting this Life forever! (*She puts down her knitting and flexes her hands. It is a very flashy, colourful "Life" she's knitting*)
Drop One It looks—ah ... kinda interesting, Purl.

Knit Who is it?
Purl Elizabeth Taylor.
Drop One (*nodding solemnly*) Then you *have* been knitting it for ever!
Knit So what's Liz gonna do next?
Purl Let's find out! I'll give the Wheel of Fortune a spin!
Drop One (*clapping her hands excitedly, like a little girl*) Oooh! Yes! Yes! Maybe she'll get married again!

They uncover the "Wheel of Fortune" and Purl gives it a spin. The wheel stops with the arrow pointing to "Cast off"

All (*reading; very disappointed*) "Cast off"!
Knit Oh, that's a shame, Purl.
Purl Yeah. I liked her Life.
Drop One It was really colourful...
Knit Not like this one. (*She holds up a coarse piece of knitting on large needles. It is a nasty drab colour and has no redeeming features*)
Purl Yuk! Who's that!?
Drop One (*raising her hand like a schoolchild*) I know! I know!
Knit Can't you guess?
Purl Princess Wanda!
Drop One (*pouting childishly, muttering*) I knew that. I knew that.
Knit (*wearily*) Yes indeed. Princess Wanda.
Purl *The* Princess Wanda?
Drop One (*cattily*) The nastiest girl in the kingdom!
Knit Isn't it hideous!?
Purl Pity you can't cast Princess *Wanda* off, instead of Liz Taylor!
Drop One (*petulantly*) Yeah. No-one would miss *her*.
Knit (*thoughtfully tapping her chin with a finger*) Hmm... (*She pauses*) You know, I just *might*...
Purl (*rather shocked*) But you'll spin first, won't you? (*She indicates the "Wheel of Fortune"*)
Drop One (*piously*) We're always meant to spin before we knit.
Knit Oh phooey! I'm sick of spinning! Yep, I think I *will* cast Wanda off!
Purl Go on, Knit. I dare you to!

Drop One fumbles, tut-tuts, mutters, giggles

Drop One ...Uh-oh! Poor Jonathan! Aren't I a knitwit! (*She stands and tosses the knitting on her stool*)
Knit Oh, don't worry, Drop One. Que...
Purl Sera...
Drop One Sera!

Act I, Scene 6

Song 5 (The Three Fates)

After this jazzy quickstep number they are wheeled off L by the Chorus

SCENE 6

The Royal Heir Beauty Salon

The Chorus set the stage as required then exit L

Song 6 (Narcissus and Hercules)

Narcissus enters R, singing

He catches sight of himself and goes from mirror to mirror preening as he sings

Near the end of the chorus, Hercules enters US through revolving doors and joins in

They get the audience to sing the chorus through again with them, conducting them

Narcissus So you're off then, are ya, Herc?
Hercules Sure am. (*He looks about furtively*) Those Cheerleaders are drivin' me nuts. (*He listens*) Uh-oh! (*He looks around, thinking he hears them*) Are those my fans?

Narcissus looks around too, then shakes his head, puzzled

Narcissus No; they're my hair-driers…
Hercules (*giving him a sideways look*) So, a beauty salon, huh?
Narcissus Sure is. And here comes our royal client; fresh from her Royal Royal Jelly Facial; Princess Wanda!

Zoë and Chloë wheel in the Princess from L. Wanda is lying back in the wheeled salon armchair. Her face is hidden by a bright blue "mudpack" mask. She has a slice of cucumber on each eye and her hair is in curlers. She wears a big pink hairdressing bib around her neck. She is not at her best! Grapes and biscuits are beside her chair

Zoë and Chloë continue her pedicure as she is positioned C

The Chorus enter L *and look on*

Gingernut enters and sits crosslegged, bored, on the floor to one side, trying to check his wing size in a hand mirror

Wanda Jeepers creepers what a dump! Where's the bubbly? (*She waves a biscuit*) I've got nothing to dunk my gingernuts in.
Narcissus Oh sorry, sorry, your Highness. Our new staff haven't turned up yet…! (*Conspiratorally*) I've ordered a set of those kinky slaves—"As advertised on TV". Only £50 a set. (*He grins, flexes his fingers and rubs his hands together*) Plus handling fee!
Wanda Huh! Slaves! Both *mine* are two grapes short of a bunch! Aren't you, Whatsername!? (*She kicks with the foot that's being pedicured by Zoë, knocking her over*) Oi! Huey? (*She kicks the other foot*) Dewey?
Zoë Zoë and Chloë. (*Automatically apologising*) Sorry, your Highness.
Wanda (*rudely mimicking her*) "Sorry, your Highness…" (*She attacks*) Remind me to fire you when we get home.
Chloë (*calmly*) You already have, your Highness.
Wanda Well, I'm not surprised. (*To all*) So … am I going to look gorgeous!?

The Chorus is conducted by Zoë and Chloë, and sound expressionless, as if they have learnt it by rote

Chorus Gosh yes your Highness, may we say
You're looking lovelier each day…

They take a quick breath, about to continue

Wanda (*halting their set piece*) Yeah, yeah, yeah. That'll do. Buzz off and write me another eulogy… I'm sick of that one.

The Chorus, Zoë and Chloë all exit L

Jeepers creepers I'm bored! I wish some rich raunchy royal would come and take me away from all this!

Hercules, Narcissus and Gingernut have been watching this. As she is still sitting with her eyes covered, Wanda doesn't know Hercules is there. He steps forward

Hercules (*speaking right into her ear, smiling*) So, Wanda, you're looking for a man to marry, huh?
Wanda (*shrieking*) Aaaaaah! A man! (*She peels the cucumber slices off her*

Act I, Scene 6   17

eyes) Huh! I wouldn't marry any of you local Greek geeks if you were ...
Hercules himself! Who *are* you, anyway?
Hercules (*very straight*) Hercules himself.
Wanda (*scornfully*) Oh yeah? And I'm Madonna. (*She sees him properly at last, and does a double take as she sees it really is Hercules*)
Hercules (*straight-faced*) Hi, Madonna. (*He turns to Narcissus*) Well, gotta go, Narc.
Narcissus (*ingratiatingly*) He really *is* Hercules, your Highness.
Wanda (*standing and glaring at Hercules*) I don't care if you *are* Hercules—you're certainly not *my* kind of guy! (*Snootily*) I'm looking for a man I can fold away and stow under the bed... (*She looks at the audience*) When not in use!
Hercules (*like a frontman on an infomercial*) And that's not all! The first twenty callers will receive a genuine one hundred per cent bonded steel *muzzle* for their pet man, *absolutely free*! (*He laughs*)
Wanda How dare you laugh at me, Mr High-and-Mighty Hercules! (*She stamps*) I think you're the most horrible, rude, beastly, obnoxious...
Hercules (*blandly*) I've enjoyed meeting you too, Wanda. (*He salutes her cheerily as he turns to leave*)
Wanda (*flying into a rage and stamping her feet*) Princess Wanda! Princess Wanda! Don't you ever *dare* to speak to me again, do you hear?

Pause

Well? Answer me!
Hercules (*ignoring her completely*) See ya, Narc. Like the ends of my hair said, "I gotta split"! (*He smiles*) A little beauty salon humour for ya there, Narc! (*He nods his head, indicating Wanda*) Your idea of Easy Street sure is different from mine.

Narcissus walks him to the main doors. They high five

Hercules leaves through the revolving doors and exits UL

Narcissus waves goodbye from the doorway

Gryphon (*going to Wanda; can't keep quiet any longer*) Well, I'm s-sorry, but that was *disgraceful*!
Wanda (*going to sit down again*) For once I agree! Hercules or no Hercules, he's got no right to talk to me like that.
Gryphon No, I ... m-mean *you* were disgraceful, Wanda. (*To a child*) Didn't *you* think so? Would you talk to Hercules like that? (*To another child*) You wouldn't talk to *anyone* like that, would you!? (*He elicits a "no" from the*

audience, then gets them to call out again much louder because he could hardly hear them) See, Wanda, everyone says you were way out of line.
Wanda (*jumping up again*) "Out of line"!? ME!? ME!? Nobody tells me how to behave. NOBODY!! DO YOU HEAR!?

Narcissus returns to them

Narcissus (*wincing and wiggling his finger in his ear*) It'd be hard not to.
Gryphon (*bravely*) Sometimes Friends have to tell Friends what they think.
Wanda (*menacingly*) And sometimes Friends have to decide whether they want to live to see their next birthday...

There is a silence. They stand belligerently, nose to beak

Narcissus (*tactfully coming between them*) Um, I think your curlers are ready, your Highness. (*He calls*) Auntie!! Auntie!! Curlers ready! (*To the audience*) Have you met my auntie yet? No? Ooh, well, you're in for a bit of a shock. (*He explains*) I wouldn't exactly say she's ugly ... but last year she had her face lifted and the doctors had to put it back again... (*He pulls a face*) It seems there was another one just like it underneath! Uh-oh, here she comes; the Auntie from *The X-Files*!

Spooky music

Medusa enters from R *She is an awesome figure, very over the top*

She fancies herself as quite a fashion plate. She swans on in high heels, mimicking a model on a catwalk ... and trips

Medusa (*falling*) Whoops! An air pocket!

Swannee whistle and snare-drum as she falls. Medusa rights herself quickly, tut-tuts and waves her finger at the bandleader, ticking him off in a flirtatious manner

(*To the bandleader*) Do you know—you're a very cheeky boy!? (*She hauls her turban, bra, etc. back into position in a very unladylike manner*)
Bandleader Um, how does it go? (*He grins*) Give me the key and I'll come in!
Medusa (*to the audience*) Ooooo, isn't he a one! (*She spies Wanda and dives into a deep curtsy. In a plummy voice*) My dear young Highness, may I say you have never looked lovelier.
Wanda (*crossly*) No, you may *not*—I've still got my curlers in.

Act I, Scene 6

Medusa We'll soon fix that! (*Cheerily*) Narcissuuuus! (*To the audience*) Have you met my nephew yet? You have!? Ah, that boy's been like a son to me! (*She pauses*) Ungrateful, rude, lazy... Actually he's smarter than he looks. (*She gives him a sideways look*) Mind you, he'd have to be!

She beams, clasping her hands as Narcissus comes over to her

Narcissus! There you are, my boy! Curler time! (*She warbles as she executes a little highland fling*) Come on! You take the high road and I'll take the low road!

Narcissus proceeds to take out the curlers on top and Medusa those at the bottom—they are not as careful as they could be! Medusa whistles cheerfully to herself as she works, drowning out Wanda's yelps and howls of protest. She has some fun attempting goal-shooting, throwing the curlers over her shoulder, between her legs, etc., aiming for a conchshell bowl that Narcissus waves around as he goes

(*Grinning*) Michael Jordon, eat ya heart out! (*She brushes out Wanda's hair*) There now, don't we look beee-oooo-tiful!

Wanda grabs the handmirror from Narcissus who has been admiring himself in it. She looks at herself

Wanda WE!? (*Rudely*) Well, I do. (*She picks sulkily at her hair*) Puh! Is this the best you can do? I told you I wanted hair to *die* for.

Medusa, behind Wanda, flexes her hands. She could happily throttle her client

Medusa (*smiling evilly at the audience*) I'm sure that could be arranged, my dear...
Narcissus (*warningly*) Auntie...!!
Wanda (*to Narcissus*) I distinctly told that wacky old bat that I want to look like Liz Hurley... (*She points rudely at Medusa*) I bet *she* makes sure *her* hair gets the best treatment.
Medusa (*patting her turban*) You want hair like *mine*, do you, my dear? (*She smiles her wicked smile*) Now that's another thing altogether. Isn't it, Narcissus?
Narcissus (*grinning*) Actually, it's a *lot* of other things altogether!
Medusa (*thoughtfully*) My hair *does* have plenty of "movement"...
Narcissus (*enjoying himself*) Yeah! It's naturally *coiling*!!
Wanda (*annoyed*) Well, stop waffling about and let's see it then.

Medusa pulls off her turban. Instead of hair she has a head full of snakes, all a-quiver

Snakes alive!! *(She jerks back as if she's been bitten)*
Narcissus Exactly!
Medusa *(stepping forward to the audience)* Yes, *you too* can have hair like this. *(She holds up some shampoo and parodies a TV commercial)* "It won't happen overnight but it *will* happen"!
Wanda Yuk! It had better not! *(Aside)* Dippy old duck...!

Medusa looks murderous and advances on Wanda again

Narcissus *(warningly, stepping between them)* Now, Auntie! You promised! Don't do anything rash!!
Wanda Yeah, don't get your toga in a twist! *(She stabs a finger at Medusa, rudely)* Hey, just who *are* you, anyway?
Medusa *(drawing herself up regally)* I am known as—Medusa!
Wanda MEDUSA! The lady with snakes instead of hair! *(Shocked)* You can turn people into stone just by... *(she gasps)* looking ... at them! *(She shields her face, turning away from Medusa)*
Narcissus *(aside)* But *you* needn't worry, Wanda. Like, you're surely stone already!
Wanda *(sharply, to Narcissus)* What was that?
Narcissus Um, I said... *(ingratiatingly)* you're like Sharon Stone already...! *(He gives her a double thumbs-up. Aside)* Whew!
Medusa Yes, indeed. One look from my snakes can turn you to stone... *(She advances menacingly on Wanda, hissing)* Especially if I'm sick of some sulky little snip of a miss's snide insinuations...
Wanda *(crying out nervously)* Look, keep your hat on, lady! *(She stumbles off hurriedly)* I... I'm off for a spell on the sunbed. Oi, Zoë! Chloë! Come on—come on—come on already!! *(She regains her composure. Very regally)* Gingernut, I'll let you stay with me and feed me my grapes...
Gryphon *(shrugging to the audience)* Gee, thanks.

Zoë and Chloë gather grapes, biscuits, etc. and wheel Wanda out R through the sunroom exit

(To the audience) Whew! It's harder than I thought. Do *you* think I should still try to be Wanda's friend? *(To a child)* Did you say *"yes"*? I really *do* want to fly, and it seems this is the only way... I suppose you're right. If Friends give up so easily, they're not really Friends, are they!? *(With a big sigh)* Oh well; here goes!

Gryphon trots off reluctantly after the three girls

Act I, Scene 6   21

Medusa and Narcissus are left on stage, on either side of the chair

Narcissus (*laughing*) Ooh, Auntie! You know you can't turn people to stone any more! Um... (*He eyes the snakes nervously*) Though, better put your hat back on, just in case...
Medusa My poor little poppets need a breather sometimes, you know. (*She turns on him*) They still haven't recovered from that terrible perm you gave me last week. (*She stabs him in the chest with her finger*) I'm not letting *you* play with me snakes and adders again. Why, this morning I got caught in the rain; and found me vipers weren't working... (*She strokes her snakes soothingly*)
Narcissus Sorry, Auntie. I *am* trying...
Medusa Yes; very. I'm still awfully attractive to men, you know. I had a very hot date last night! (*She wets her lips with an open mouth*)
Narcissus Did it burn your tongue!?
Medusa (*preening*) I turned a few heads, I can tell you!
Narcissus (*aside*) And a few stomachs...!!
Medusa (*smiling into the mirror*) I'm certainly not too old for dating.
Narcissus Right, Auntie. (*Aside*) *Carbon* dating!
Medusa (*fluttering her lashes*) You've got to help me recapture me lost youth, Narcissus.
Narcissus (*cheekily*) I think he's hiding over there... (*He points to a young male in the audience*)
Medusa Oh, you cheeky monkey! (*She belts him with a mirror, then replaces her turban*)

Narcissus looks relieved. He holds up the mirror to help her tuck it all in. She addresses a snake as she tucks it away

Under you go, Monty, good boy. (*She's finished*) There. One day I expect you to be a Top Beauty Consultant like me.
Narcissus One day I expect to be a *better* Beauty Consultant than you!
Medusa *You*, Narcissus? Why, you're so lazy, even your *threats* are idle!
Narcissus Don't forget I passed all my Beauty School tests last year, Auntie. (*He counts them off on his fingers in a rhythm*) Waxing, frosting, crimping, plucking, tinting, teasing, liposucking... (*Cockily*) So now I can do anything *you* can do, Auntie. And just as well. (*Brightly*) Or better!
Medusa Oh no, you can't!
Narcissus Oh yes, I can!
Medusa (*eliciting audience support*) Oh no, you can't!
Narcissus (*eliciting audience support*) Oh yes, I can!

They repeat this procedure till they get a good response

Medusa (*quietening the audience*) Let's see then! (*She touches her false eyelashes*) Can you tint an eyelash?
Narcissus (*nodding confidently*) Yep! Quick as a flash! (*On the attack*) Can you do a french plait?
Medusa (*snapping her fingers*) Huh! Just like that!

During the intro to the song, Narcissus sits in the chair and scoots it DS *while Medusa wheels forward a trayful of props*

Song 7 (Medusa and Narcissus)

This song should involve plenty of funny props. See Production Notes for suggested business. The number finishes with Medusa standing on the chair, towering over Narcissus like the Statue of Liberty

Zoë enters from sunroom R *in a terrible state, carrying a scroll*

Zoë (*entering*) The Princess has gone!!

Chloë enters

Chloë (*rushing in behind Zoë*) They've taken her away!!
Zoë ⎫
Chloë ⎭ (*together*) Wanda's been kidnapped!!
Medusa (*making a big business of getting a piggyback down from Narcissus*) Huh! Who'd want to kidnap *her*?
Zoë ⎫
Chloë ⎭ (*together*) CYCLOPS!!
Narcissus Cyclops!?
Medusa Cyclops the giant!?
Chloë His soldiers have taken her!
Zoë And Gingernut too!

Narcissus takes the scroll from Zoë and reads it. He holds it up. We see the sign of a single big, red eye on the back of it. He reads the note aloud

Narcissus "My Red Guards have Princess Wanda! She will be my bride. Death to Hercules if he comes to her rescue! Signed: Cyclops." (*He taps the "red eye"*) Yep; that's from old Red-Eye!
Medusa This won't look good in the *Sunday Smut*! (*Dramatically she waves her arms to indicate huge headlines*) "Wanda whipped away in hairdressing horror". Narcissus, you've got to find her!

Narcissus doesn't look very keen

Act I, Scene 7

Go get 'em!
Narcissus So much for Easy Street.

Narcissus runs out R then returns

There's no sign of them!
Medusa (*pointing to the street*) Then get Hercules. He's our only hope!

Narcissus races out the revolving doors then straight back in, in one continuous motion

Narcissus But Hercules'll be at the airport by now! He shot off like Ben Hur on Prozac!
Medusa Then grab a taxi and follow him! He's got a chariot phone, hasn't he?

Narcissus races out the door then straight in again, screeching to a halt

Narcissus (*arms flailing in the air*) But Cyclops will kill him! (*He stops and thinks*) But we can't let our best client be kidnapped!

Narcissus runs out again—then re-enters in the same movement

Yet we can't send Hercules to his death! (*He stops and thinks*) A kidnapping would be awful publicity for us!

Narcissus runs out again, re-entering immediately

But there's no such thing as bad publicity... (*He stops and thinks*)
Medusa Narcissus! (*Threateningly*) I will take off my hat...!!
Narcissus Snakes alive!

Narcissus gives her a horrified look, and rushes out into the street, followed by Medusa and the servants. All exit UL

Scene 7

Frontcloth. The Red Guards

The Chorus enter and take up their positions L

They can deliver the following in two or three groups, two lines of verse each, all gossiping

Chorus   My goodness! What exciting news;
The Princess has been captured!
Imagine being Cyclop's bride
I bet she's not enraptured!
He's had his evil eye on her
Since she was just a nipper!
I think I'd rather tie the Marriage
Knot with Jack the Ripper!! (*They look out into the audience*)

During the following the Red Guards enter from the back of the auditorium

Full Chorus But here they come; no time to ponder
The fate of Gingernut ... and Wanda!

The Chorus scurries off L *and exits*

The Red Guards proceed down the aisles, "threatening" people with their swords as they make their way to the stage. They chant "Hooh-hah!! Hooh-hah!" kung fu style as they go

Song 8 (Rap by Leader of the Red Guards)

At the end of the song all exit L, *except the Leader of the Guards and one Guard who exit* R

The Guards return with Wanda and Gryphon who are led on from R. *Their hands are in manacles in front of them, attached to chains held by the Leader and the Guard*

Wanda (*furiously*) Talk about a Bad Hair Day!! It's all your fault, Gingernut! Some Friend *you* turned out to be!
Gryphon (*stuttering badly in his distress, finding it very hard to get the words out*) It's n-not my f-f-fault! You're b-being p-p-positively b-b-beastly to me...
Wanda (*very briskly*) That's easy for *you* to say! (*She pauses as she considers this statement*) Anyway, *you* don't have to marry that ugly big one-eyed brute—*I* do! (*She sighs*) It's a high price to pay for being beautiful and popular.
Leader (*smirking*) So *you're* Princess Wanda.
Guard (*sneeringly*) *The* Princess Wanda. (*He conducts the audience to join in*) The nastiest girl in the kingdom!!

They think it's a big joke

Act I, Scene 8

Wanda (*looking around, shocked*) Who says that?
Leader Everybody says that. (*He points to the audience*) You heard them!
Wanda (*stunned*) Do people really say that about me? (*She looks as if she will cry*)
Gryphon (*putting his arm around Wanda*) Well, I'm not going to ever again. (*To the audience*) Wanda's my Friend, isn't she, everyone? (*Kindly*) So from now on I won't let anyone be mean to you.
Wanda Why, thank you, Gingernut. Nobody's ever stuck up for me before.
Leader Get a move on, girlie. (*He pokes his spear at them. Leering*) We don't want to keep Cyclops waiting, do we!?
Wanda Poor Daddy. (*With a big breath*) When he hears that I've been kidnapped by an evil giant with only one eye who lives in an underground cave and is forcing me to marry him so he can keep me down there with him for the rest of my life ... what will poor Daddy say!?
Leader (*very snidely*) "What took ya so long!?"

Music: Band Reprise of Song 8

They exit L, *with Wanda and the Gryphon being dragged off by their chains*

SCENE 8

The Palace

This is a full stage scene. The palace should have a sweeping staircase US *from which grand entrances will be made*

A stand set DS *has a working microphone which the King uses*

The King's bodyguards stand sternly, arms folded, around the perimeter. The King will interact with the band, as they are his "group". He counts the band in

The King (*pointing to the band*) Ah one. Ah two. Ah one, two, three.

Song 9 (The King)

The Chorus will be the backing group for this number. (See Costume Suggestions.) They will be in position behind the King and perform with suitable handjive movements. As the song continues, they can, in the excitement of the number, pair up with the bodyguards and rock'n'roll together. During the song the King will gyrate and throw a towel to a girl in the audience as a souvenir. The sound of screaming fans will be heard when this happens and again at the end of song, more screaming fans

(*Bowing to the audience, waving to them etc.; drawling, Southern style*) Bless you. Now remember you-all—The King *lives*!!
Bandleader The King lives!! (*He gets the band and the audience to echo this*) Long live the King!!

This is also echoed by the band and the audience. We hear a man screaming as if he is being murdered

The King (*shouting up to the sound or lighting box*) Hey, mister! That's the wrong reckid!
Voice From Box Sorry. How's this?

Fans screaming

The King (*beaming*) Aw, now that's music to mah ears. (*He mops his brow on a towel*)

Narcissus rushes in via the staircase

The King's bodyguards dash over and seize Narcissus on either side. They frog-march him up to the King who looks him up and down. He waves the bodyguards away. They take up positions at the sides until their song

Say, boy; are you a fan?
Narcissus No, I'm a hairdresser.

Medusa rushes on behind him, in best turban and a fur stole

The King (*looking Medusa up and down*) So what're *you*? A *cross*-dresser?

During the following, Narcissus bobs about in the background, trying to get a word in edgeways

Medusa (*adjusting her bosom*) I, sir, am *all woman*! (*She straightens her turban*) And more... (*She purses her lips sensuously at him*) I'm so thrilled to meet you! The King himself! I am *rapt*! (*She curtsies elaborately and kisses his ring*)
The King (*fingering her stole*) Yeah, ma'am; but what in; dead muskrat?
Medusa (*defensively*) This is a *stimulated* mink. No living creature suffered for this garment. (*She winks at the King*) Except me!

Act I, Scene 8

The King (*puzzled*) But why the towel on your head, ma'am?
Medusa That's my best turban. (*She pats it*) Isn't it gorgeous! Whenever I'm down in the dumps I get myself a new hat.
Narcissus (*eyes wide*) Is *that* where you get them!?

Medusa rises, looking daggers at him

(*To King*) Listen, King! We're Princess Wanda's hairdressers! There's been a disaster!
The King (*disturbed*) Don't tell me lil Wanda's got split ends!
Narcissus (*urgently*) Worse! She's been kidnapped...
Medusa By this weird creepy jerk who plans to marry her...
The King Not Michael Jackson!? (*He flings up his arms in horror*)

"Ta-dah" drum payoff for punchline

Narcissus (*very patiently*) No sir, not Michael Jackson. Wanda's been kidnapped by a big ugly brute who's terrorized the country for years with his cruel attacks on innocent people...
Medusa He's mean! (*She snarls and makes claw-hands*)
Narcissus He's mad! (*He puts thumbs in his ears, and waves his fingers*)
Medusa He's one-eyed! (*She makes one big "eye" on her forehead with her hands, then makes it "wink"*)
The King (*absolutely appalled*) Not Michael *Heseltine*!?!?
Medusa ⎫ (*together; losing patience with him*) No, *not* Michael Heseltine!!
Narcissus ⎭ CYCLOPS!!
The King Cyclops! The *giant*!?

Narcissus and Medusa nod vigorously

Narcissus But look who I got here to help you!

Cheerleaders burst in down the staircase, waving pompoms

One Give us an "H"!
Two Give us an "E"!
Three Give us an "R"!
Four Give us a "C"!
Five Give us a "U"!
Six "L"!
Seven "E"!
Eight "S"!
All HERCULES!

They repeat this with Narcissus encouraging the audience to join in the chant

>*They end up forming an aisle for Hercules who enters at the top of the staircase and makes a muscleman pose, then bounds down to take up another pose* C

>*Two bodyguards lunge at him from each side. Hercules holds them at arms length as they try futilely to apprehend him, then tosses them aside with an easy flick of his hands. He goes up to the King*

The King Hercules!
Hercules The King!
The King ⎫
Hercules ⎭ (*together*) Hey, I always wanted to meet you, man!

>*They slap each other on the shoulder like "good ol buddies" whereupon the King has to be helped to his feet by the bodyguards*

Hercules My friend here tells me you need my help.
The King (*holding both of Hercules's hands, sincerely*) Herc, can you bring my lil Wanda back to her Daddy?
Hercules No problem. I'll cancel my flight!
The King (*indicating the shrine*) Ma dear old Momma used to say—bless her heart—"If the good Lord had wanted us to fly, he'd've given us wheels"...

>*They all ponder this for a minute*

Hercules Yeah. Well. Anyways, you can count on me, King.
The King You bring my lil Wanda back home safe and she's yours to have and to hold from that day on.
Hercules (*looking horrified*) You mean, like, *marry* her.
The King (*clasping both Hercules's hands*) I do, boy. I purely do.
Hercules (*in a frenzy, pulling away*) Hey, man. I couldn't do that! (*He pushes Narcissus in front as if for protection*) Narc, tell him! I wouldn't marry Wanda if she... (*He stops*)

>*The King does not like what he is hearing*

   I mean... (*He acts very cool*) That's really big of you, King. But ... ah... I can't accept.
The King Why not?
Hercules Don't get me wrong, but if I find a gal to marry, let me tell you what she'll be like...

Act I, Scene 8

Song 10 (Hercules)

The King (*nodding*) True, that don't sound much like ma lil Wanda…
Hercules Well, we'll get her back for ya, King. (*He turns to go*) Come on, Narc. We're outa here!
Narcissus What!? *Me* too?
Hercules You betya it's you too! We got us a Thirteenth Labour!
Narcissus Hey, Herc; ever heard the sayin' that thirteen's an unlucky number?
Hercules Hey, Narc; ever heard the sayin' that Narcissus is more chicken than KFC?

Song 11 (Hercules, Narcissus, Medusa, King, Greek Chorus, Cheerleaders and Bodyguards)

CURTAIN

ACT II

Scene 1

The Royal Heir Beauty Salon

There are salon counters but no chairs. Two hair-trolleys on wheels contain various doctored props e.g. basin, foam, etc.

Medusa enters L on rollerblades. She hurtles across the stage, arms windmilling for balance, and straight off the other side. There she grabs a broom and returns, pushing it before her and sweeping as she sings

Song 12 (Medusa)

Medusa does a circuit of the stage, then collapses in a sprawl C, legs up so we can see her bloomers. She puffs, then fans her face with a tiny battery-driven propellor fan which she retrieves from down her bosom. She then uses it to cool each armpit and is about to stick it up her bloomers when she looks up at the audience

Medusa (*seeing all those people watching her*) Ooops! (*To the audience*) Whew! This'll be the death of me! But I must keep fit now I've found meself a man! And oooh isn't he scrrrrrumptious! (*She clutches her bosom dramatically*) Be still my foolish heart! (*She caresses a feather duster erotically over her face*) Kingy! Kingy! I am as play dough in your Royal Hands. (*She sighs in a lovesick manner then proceeds to fluff round half-heartedly with the duster. She stops*) I hope Narcissus has ordered those new slaves for me. He can't just potter off and expect me to run the place on my own. (*She stops and listens as the music begins*)

Music 13

As music starts, she sits R and takes off her gloves so she can remove her skateboots. She sniffs and makes a face. She does the same with her football socks, takes air freshener from the counter by her and sprays her feet, socks and surrounding air lavishly. Then she takes her shoes from her pinny pocket and puts them on. This business carries on through the dance after she has seen enough of it

Act II, Scene 1

Narcissus struts on from L *with huge high goosestep strides. He is extremely arrogant throughout this dance*

The Slaves enter DS *in a straight line, dancing in a high-kicking Irish style*

Medusa scrabbles backwards awkwardly across the floor as they advance on her. The slaves must perform like very energetic machines. At the end of the dance they finish with one leg raised, which they stamp down on Narcissus's command. Then they go through the final sequence of the dance again, ending with the stamp once more. They are about to do this a third time when they are interrupted by Medusa who whistles at them through her fingers like a farmer. She flaps the gloves at her nephew and then replaces them

Oi! You! Michael *Flatfeet*! Did you hear what happened to the Irish tap dancer!?
Narcissus (*puffing*) No. What happened to the Irish tap dancer?
Medusa He fell into the sink!! (*To the audience*) *Tap* dancer. *Sink*. Get it!? Oh, please yourselves...
Narcissus (*groaning*) Oh, Auntie, give us a break! (*Brightly, to the audience*) Hey, they're pretty cool, aren't they!

He gestures proudly to the slaves who dance off into a large semi-circle around the back of the stage and stand like robots, awaiting his instructions

When I've gone, they'll do all the work I did!
Medusa (*scathingly*) A ninety-six year-old one-armed *dwarf* could do all the work *you* did! And speaking of "going", when *are* you?
Narcissus Now! Oh, but we've got something very important to do before I go.
Medusa Oooh yes! The lucky winners! (*To the audience*) Hands up if you received a Lucky Voucher at half-time? That's right, hold it up and show me. Oooh, they're a stroppy-looking lot, Narcissus. Are you sure you gave them to the right people?
Narcissus Yes, Auntie. They were all sitting in the lucky seats, like you said.
Medusa (*going into the audience and looking them over with a huge magnifying glass*) At least they've got hair. (*Possibly examining a bald head*) Well, some of them. (*She points to a boy who looks suitable*) You, sonny. You can come up. (*She gets him on stage*) What's your name? (*She repeats it for the audience*)
Narcissus Hold up your Lucky Vouchers! (*To a girl who looks suitable*) Right, and *you* can come on up with me. (*He leads the girl onstage beside the boy*) And your name is? (*He repeats it for the audience*) [Girl's name] and [Boy's name], our Lucky Voucher winners have won... (*he takes one*

of their vouchers and reads) ..."an amazing free makeover!! As seen on TV!! At the Royal Heir Beauty Salon, the crowning glory of the crowned heads of [name of town]".

Medusa Well, aren't you the lucky ones!? Let's give [children's names] a big hand!

She pulls an outsize stuffed or polystyrene "hand" out of the wings and presents it to one child then the other so they "shake hands" with it while Narcissus encourages the audience to applaud

Right! Two Emergency Makeovers coming up! Chair, Narcissus!

Narcissus snaps his fingers and the slaves tap-dance off in two groups, one to each side, returning with two chairs which they place c

The children sit in the chairs and the slaves return to the sides where they wait motionless, arms at sides. Medusa goes to the boy, looks at him and does a double take of exaggerated horror

Blimey! (*She examines him closely with the magnifying glass, holding it so the audience get a distorted view of the boy*) This one's going to need an awful lot of work. Look at his hair! Look at his fingernails! Look at his face!

Narcissus (*putting a big bib on the girl in her chair and looking at her dubiously*) This one's not much better! Where do we start, Auntie?

Medusa At the top end I suppose. I think this is it. (*She examines the boy's chin through her magnifying glass*) Oooooh, [child's name]! (*Accusingly*) You haven't shaved today, have you? (*She gets the boy to answer "no"*) I've seen smoother chins on a hedgehog! Narcissus! (*She snaps her fingers*) Bib!

Narcissus They're over there. (*He nods towards the back*) In the Greek Urn. (*He indicates an urn at the back*)

Medusa What's a Greek Urn?

Narcissus About two dollars an hour!! (*He strikes a "ta-dah" pose*)

Drum payoff

(*To the audience*) An oldie but a goodie!

Medusa (*like Captain Mainwaring in* Dad's Army) Stupid boy. (*She looks in the urn*) There's nothing in it.

Narcissus (*indicating the bib on the girl*) They must be all in the wash, Auntie.

Medusa (*gleefully, punching the air*) Yay! I've always wanted an excuse to do this... (*She proceeds to strip*)

Act II, Scene 1   33

Music

When Medusa begins to strip the bandleader realises what she is up to, grins and bursts into appropriate music as if spontaneously. Medusa plays up to it and—sexily—removes her rubber gloves finger by finger as she eyes a male in the audience. She twirls each glove before tossing it at him. She then removes her housecoat, teasingly undoing and doing up the ties, slowly slipping it from one shoulder and then the other until finally she sheds the housecoat to reveal an awful lurid, frilly petticoat and long drawers

(*Pointing saucily to the man she's vamped*) Eat your heart out, Sonny. That's as far as I go without a safety net!

The band continues to play The Stripper

Oi! (*She whistles between her fingers at the band*) Tortelli! Put a sock in it. And if you don't I'll put one in for you. (*Aside*) With me foot still wearing it! (*She holds up the housedress to Narcissus*) See, I'll use me pinny for a bib. Nice, innit!? I bought it at [local store] for an absolutely *ridiculous* figure!

Narcissus (*grinning; to the audience*) Yes; *yours*!!
Medusa Oi! Watch it! I'm going to run rings round you with my beauty tricks!
Narcissus Oh no, you won't.
Medusa Oh yes, I will.
Narcissus (*soliciting the audience to join in*) Oh no, you won't!
Medusa (*soliciting the audience to join in*) Oh yes, I will!

This is repeated once or twice with the audience encouraged to shout as loudly as they can. Medusa blows a percing whistle

To work!

Music: Background reprise of Song 7

The music continues through part of the make-overs

Medusa ties the pinny around the boy's neck with a flourish and takes a basin and a towel from the hair-trolley. She sprays "shaving foam" on the boy's cheeks and chin. It is actually an aerosol of whipped cream. Then she takes a "cut-throat razor" from the basin and makes a few swashbuckling passes in the air with it

This'll tickle your tonsils. (*To the boy*) Now tell me something, [boy's

name]. Do you like eating? You do? Oh, well, I'd better keep your head joined on then, hadn't I! Now, we'll just test the razor. (*She holds it up to test it. The razor is soft plastic so that as she tests the "blade" it bends and proves totally blunt and useless*) It's got about as much cutting edge left as John Major... Ah well... Here goes! (*She "shaves" the boy, using a towel to wipe up, and gets some shaving foam from the can on her hands. She licks it off her finger then tries some more. It is so good she squirts some straight on to her stuck-out tongue*)
Narcissus (*sharply*) AUNTIE! That's not very nice!
Medusa Nonsense! It's delicious. Stick your tongue out. (*She squirts the can at Narcissus but it goes over his face*)

He is understandably annoyed

Narcissus (*wiping with a towel*) Stop it, Auntie! What's wrong with you?
Medusa (*waltzing around, warbling*) I'm in love, I'm in love, I'm in love, I'm in love with a wonderful guy...!!
Narcissus Pull yourself together, Auntie. Have you finished shaving [boy's name]? Then what about a haircut?
Medusa (*to the boy*) Do you want a haircut? (*She holds his head, making him nod*) Yes, he wants a haircut.
Narcissus Then give him a haircut.
Medusa What style do you think would suit him? A Kojak? (*See holds up a poster of Kojak or someone else with a completely shaven head*)
Narcissus Or a Mohawk? (*He holds up a poster of a punk*)
Medusa I know!! A Beatles haircut! (*She grabs the bowl and quickly turns it upside down on the boy's head. She snaps her fingers at the slaves*)

The Slaves jig off in two lines, one to each side. One group returns with a huge pair of scissors and the other with an old-fashioned hair-drier on a wheeled stand

(*Waving the huge pair of scissors*) Look! They're Narcissus's scissors!! (*She mops her mouth with the towel ostentatiously, after all the sissing*)

Narcissus attends to the girl

Narcissus Do you need a shave too, [girl's name]? No? You sure? But I bet you'd like a facial, wouldn't you? And a haircut? Ooh, you *are* a brave little thing! First some lovely pink cheeks! (*He applies circles of blusher on her cheeks. He will make her look pretty, but doll-like*) Gorgeous! Now a dab of lipstick. (*He puts it on in a red cupid's bow shape*) And some fabulous long eyelashes... (*He paints black "lashes" around her eyes*) Ooooh, she looks a living doll, doesn't she, Auntie!?

Act II, Scene 1   35

Medusa A little bobby dazzler, Narcissus. But what about the hair?

During the following Medusa will be clipping away around the basin busily with the outsize scissors

Narcissus A haircut! Do *you* like the Kojak look, [girl's name]? No? We could do with a change of colour, though, couldn't we? (*He takes a spray bottle from the hair-trolley*) My Magical Instant Colour Rinse! (*He holds the spray up proudly*) Right on! You'll be a beautiful blonde [or redhead ... whatever she isn't now!] in two minutes flat. (*He "sprays" her hair*) It just needs to dry. (*He snaps his fingers*)

The Slaves tap-dance around in a line positioning a hair-drier over the girl's head

Medusa Finished! (*She snaps her fingers*)

The Slaves tap-dance around the boy's chair

Drum roll

The Slaves remove the basin from the boy's head. He has indeed got a Beatles haircut

"Tah—dah!" drum payoff

Narcissus (*pointing in disgust and coming over to them*) Yuk! What are these? (*He picks a big black beetle out of the boy's hair and holds it up by one leg*)
Medusa (*pulling out another one or two; calmly*) Beetles. I told you, it's a Beatles haircut.

They hold up, by the leg, two or three nasty wriggly beetles

If you want to look your best, there's nothing like a good haircut.
Narcissus (*shaking his head*) And that's *nothing* like a good haircut. You've lost your touch, Auntie. Just look at *my* makeover! (*He snaps his fingers*)

The Slaves jig around the girl's chair to remove the hair-drier

Drum roll ... drum payoff

(*Whipping the drier off the girl's head*) Ta dah!

Narcissus is looking boastfully over at Medusa, notes her expression of horror and looks at the girl who now has bright green spiky punk hair

Medusa (*hands on hips; mockingly*) A beautiful blonde, huh?

Narcissus could kick himself

Narcissus I hate it when that happens…!

The Slaves continue jigging in a line to the back, pick up two hand mirrors and bring them over, giving one to each child to show them what they look like

Medusa (*to the audience*) Isn't my makeover just gorgeous?

She gets the boy to stand up and proudly displays him. Narcissus encourages the audience to shout "no!"

Narcissus (*to the audience*) Isn't *my* makeover absolutely fabulous?

He gets the girl to stand up and proudly displays her. Medusa encourages the audience to shout "no!"

Medusa Yay! Girlpower! Mine's the best, so there! (*She grabs a can in each hand from the trolley and holds them like pistols*)
Narcissus Snot! *Mine* is! (*He also grabs a can in each hand*)

They circle each other like gunfighters in a showdown

Medusa (*cowboy-style*) This town ain't big enough for the two of us!

Music: Band reprise, at madcap speed, of Song 7

A full-on spraying duel ensues and all rush off L

Scene 2

Frontcloth

Medusa's clean-up

Medusa enters with a mop and bucket to clean up any mess

Act II, Scene 3   37

Medusa (*to a woman in the audience*) Oooh, I just *hate* housework, don't you? You dust and sweep and scrub and polish. And a couple of months later you've got to do it all over again...!! Ooooh; I know! (*She does her famous whistle and gestures in a very unfeminine way to the wings*) Oi, you lot!!

Music: Band reprise or No. 13

The Slaves "Riverdance" on again. Medusa gives her mop to the leader, who mops the floor as they all set off in a line around the stage

Medusa watches, delighted, chatting with the audience about how clever she is until she is chased off stage by the end of the mop

SCENE 3

The River Styx

This scene plays in front of the mid-stage traveller

The Chorus enter L. They have changed their sheets

During this, Hercules and Narcissus enter through the audience, hopelessly lost

Chorus No doubt you think we're looking treats—
Today's the day we change our sheets.
And so, all clad in spotless linen
We move on from that weird beginnin'
Unto the next scene in Act Two
Where He-men do what He-men do—
To Hercules, our trusty hero
And his friend—whose IQ's zero!

Narcissus is studying a local street map. As they make their way down, they ask nearby members of the audience to point them in the right direction, until they reach the stage, R. There is a river before them, represented by watery lighting. Two of the Chorus have erected signs on stands, like AA signs. The one on the R side says "River Styx", the one on the L side says "The Other Side"

Hercules Looks like we've struck a river here, Narc.

Narcissus (*bewildered*) No kiddin'?
Hercules Is it on the map?
Narcissus (*checking the map again, it's upside down*) I dunno, Herc. It's all Greek to me.
Hercules (*taking the map from him and turning it around*) Yeah. Here it is; the River Styx. (*He reads the map*) Oh no! It's the River of No Return!
Narcissus (*to the audience*) Why do I suddenly feel worried...?
Hercules Lighten up, Narc! We just gotta find a way across, that's all.
Narcissus (*peering into the depths*) Yuk! It's filthy and full of creepy-crawlies!
Hercules I'm surprised the Council hasn't piped it into our drinking supply yet! (*He looks over to the Chorus and waves*) Hey, ladies; any ideas how we can get across?
Chorus (*rather sarcastically*) Perhaps some object that can float?
        Have you considered, well—a *boat*!?
Hercules Brilliant!
Narcissus Aaallll right!!

They high-five each other while the Chorus pull on—from L—*a small boat mounted on a truck*

(*Not impressed*) Oh great. It's the Titanic!!
Chorus (*to Hercules*) Might we suggest this more or less'll
        Suit you as regards a vessel—
        Take this craft we have before us.
        Yours, sire, compliments of the Chorus!
Narcissus (*very unhappy about crossing*) Don't accept it, Herc. Remember what they say—beware of Greeks bearing gifts!
Hercules Chill out, Narc.

They climb into the boat

(*To the Chorus*) Thanks ladies! Way to go!

The Chorus oblige by pulling the truck across the "river"

Do ya know what's on the other side of the river, ladies?
Chorus   O mighty Hercules, we dread to tell;
        The place you head for now is known as ... well...
        We tremble at the word, as highborn ladies
          The other name it goes by, sire, is (*in a stage whisper*) "Hades"!
Narcissus (*horrified*) I told ya we shouldn't've come! (*He turns around and tries frantically, with his hands, to paddle back the way they came*)

Act II, Scene 3

Hercules grabs him by the jacket and stops him

Hercules Hey, let's get this over with, huh? Thanks, gals.

By now they are at the other side

They step out and the Semi-chorus takes the boat off L

(Patronisingly, to the Chorus) You're pretty strong, considering you're the weaker sex.

The distant sound of singing is heard off L

Song 14 (The Three Fates)

What's that? Who's that singing?

During the following, the Demi-chorus emerge, this time pushing the truck on which the Three Fates sit, singing and knitting

Semi-chorus They know your Present, know your Past
They know your Future—and your mate's
Know when you're born and when you'll die—
We bring to you— *(like a TV show compere)*
The Three-ee-ee Fates!

All the Chorus exit L

The song continues. Knit and Drop One take it in turns to turn their head sharply to one side then the other to look at Purl who sits in the middle, as if they are gossiping, while they sing the words

Hercules *(shouting over them)* This could go on forever.
Narcissus Who do they think they are? The Spice Girls?

After one chorus of the song Hercules manages to butt in

Hercules Yo, gals. So you're the Three Fates, huh?

The singing stops

Knit Right on! I'm Knit! Just call me the Fate Worse Than Death! *(She draws a finger across her neck in a cut-throat gesture)*

Purl And I'm Purl. Just call me the Fickle Finger of Fate! (*She wiggles a finger flirtatiously at him*)
Drop One And I'm Drop One. Just call me... Oh-Bother-I've-Really-Gone-And-Done-It-Now! (*She's pulled all her stitches off*)
Knit Ooooh dear. Bye bye, Jonathan!
Purl Hey, you guys! Today Knit's going to *cast someone off*!
Drop One (*bouncing excitedly*) You'll never guess who!
Knit (*serenely*) I'm just about to cast off Princess Wanda, that's all!
Purl *The* Princess Wanda!
Drop One The nastiest girl in the kingdom!
Hercules WHAT!? You're doing *what*!? (*He grabs the knitting from Knit*) Whoa! You can't do that!!
The Fates Why not?
Hercules Well... (*He thinks hard*) Princess Wanda is young and beautiful...
Narcissus And rich and famous...
Knit And mean and selfish...
Purl And a jolly boring piece of knitting!
Drop One Not a good stitch to her name! (*She points to the knitting*)
Hercules (*looking*) But that's no reason to cast her off. If you do she'll die!
Knit Give me one good reason why I shouldn't.
Purl Yes. It's bad enough having to knit the *nice* ones...
Drop One (*flexing and rubbing her hands dolefully*) Oooooh! I'm getting RSI...
Hercules But surely Wanda can't be *all* bad!?
Knit Get a life, Herc! Can you think of *one* nice thing about her?
Hercules (*thinking hard*) Um. Let's see. (*He brightens*) She's... (*His face falls*) No, she's not really, is she...?
Narcissus (*brightening—he has a thought*) She's always... (*His face falls too*) No ... she's not at all, come to think of it...

They stand in hopeless silence as each idea bites the dust

Knit Tell you what. If Princess Wanda does just *one* decent thing today, I won't cast her off. OK, Herc?
Narcissus Get real! Princess *Wanda* doin' something *nice* for someone! (*He shakes his head*) Man, give us a break! (*He guffaws*)
Hercules If she does, then you'll let her live?

The Fates nod and knit

OK. Thanks. C'mon, Narc, let's blow!

The Fates reprise Song 14

Act II, Scene 4

Song 15 (Hercules and Narcissus)

The Chorus returns and wheels the Three Fates off L as the song is ending

Hercules and Narcissus exit R waving to them

Scene 4

The Mountain top

The Curtains *part to reveal Venus on the mountain top once more. Two hands are holding her big book, one is ticking off names in it and one has the wrist held up so she can see the time on her watch*

Hercules and Narcissus enter R, look around, then up as they see the mountain. They are amazed as they see Venus at the summit

Venus (*not looking up from her watch*) You took your time!
Narcissus (*holding back, staring up*) Who or what is *that*?
Hercules (*to Narcissus*) Don't worry. I'm sure she's quite *harmless.*
Narcissus (*aside, waving his arms*) Looks like she's got more than her fair share to me!
Hercules (*to Venus*) You're Venus, the Goddess of Love, right?
Venus Indeed I am, Hercules. The Three Fates said you were on your way.
Hercules You know them?
Venus Of course. We work hand in glove (*she waves each hand one by one*) and hand in glove and hand in glove and hand in glove... The Fates have decreed that it is time you met me... You, Hercules, will find your True Love today.
Narcissus (*hopefully*) Me too?
Venus Why, Narcissus, *you* have been in love for years!

He looks amazed

Ever since you looked in your first mirror!
Hercules (*laughing*) Actually, Venus, it's not *love* I'm looking for—it's Princess Wanda. She's being held prisoner by Cyclops, the one-eyed giant.
Venus Maybe he's not the only one-eyed one around here, Hercules. Have you considered that your quest for Princess Wanda and your discovery of Love might be one and the same thing?
Hercules Love! Princess Wanda! (*He looks pained*)
Venus Just remember, Hercules; Love is the most powerful force of all. Even the bravest man in the world can tremble before the Power of Love...

Song 16 (Venus)

Venus points off and waves all her arms

They exit L

SCENE 5

Frontcloth

There is a large rock L *on which Wanda is seated. The Gryphon huddles at her feet*

Gryphon Oh, Wanda, what are we going to do? How can I look after you now?
Wanda It'll be all right, Gingernut. Cheer up! (*She strokes his head fondly and we see that at last she is caring about someone other than herself*) You see, I'll look after you, my friend. Now, go to sleep.

Gingernut rests his head at her feet and sleeps

(*To herself*) Cyclops wants to marry me! (*She shudders*) Yuk! Oh, it's too awful to think about. If only there were someone who could save me... (*She looks out wistfully*) Imagine if there were someone out there who loved me ... someone ... somewhere...

Song 17 (Wanda (joined by Hercules))

Hercules enters R *during this song. He listens to her and joins in the duet without either of them seeing each other. He is falling in love with an unseen, unknown voice, little realizing it is Wanda*

At the end of this number Narcissus comes on after Hercules

Wanda exits L

Hercules Did you hear that, Narcissus? What a beautiful song! What a beautiful voice! What a beautiful girl!
Narcissus How do you know that? You didn't even see her!
Hercules I didn't need to see her, Narc. I felt her ... in my heart. (*Awestruck*) Now I know what the Goddess meant by the "Power of Love". I *will* find True Love ... here ... today.

Act II, Scene 5

Narcissus But where is she, Herc? *Who* is she?
Hercules Have faith, Narcissus. I will know before the day is out. But first things first. We must find Wanda.

The Semi-chorus enter L

Semi-chorus Love 'em or hate 'em you must admit
Those crazy Fates they sure can knit.
They're knitting up a storm right now
'Cause Wanda's changed her ways ... and how!
One final time we'll wheel 'em out
And see what this is all about.

The Demi-chorus once more wheel in the Three Fates, seated on their stools knitting. The "Wanda" life that Knit was knitting now has bright pretty colours added at the most recent part. Drop One is dozing over her knitting

Knit (*to the Chorus*) Ta, girls! You're doing great.
Purl We're on! Drop One! Wake up!
Drop One (*awaking with a start*) I wasn't asleep. I was just looking at the inside of my eyelids for a minute...
Knit You know, suddenly the weirdest thing's happened to this Life! Look!! (*She holds up Wanda's life; now quite beautiful*)
Purl (*astounded*) You're never going to tell us that's You-Know-Who!
Drop One (*pettishly*) Well *I* don't know who. WHO!?
Knit (*casually, ready to enjoy their reaction*) It's only Princess Wanda...!!
Purl (*amazed*) *The* Princess Wanda?
Drop One The nastiest girl——
Knit (*interrupting*) No! That's just the point! She's *not* nasty! Look at her!
Purl That's really Princess Wanda!?
Drop One You're kidding!
Knit *She's* not meant to change her Fate—*I* am.
Purl You'll have to alter the whole pattern of her Life!!
Drop One That's incredible! She must've actually done something nice!
Knit (*wonderingly*) So I won't be casting her off tonight.
Purl Can Mere Mortals choose their own Fate now, without us?
Drop One Nah! They'll always need *us* to blame, when things go wrong!

Song 18 (The Three Fates)

As this is their final song and dance this must be a big number with a high kicking finale, Rockettes style

They dance off R

The Chorus hurries on and removes the deserted truck

Scene 6

Cyclops' Grotto

Music: Sabre Dance—Demons' dance

This is a full-stage scene, smoky, subterranean and spooky. Two upright poles are placed DR

Wanda is bound to one and Gingernut to the other. The Red Guards stand in line on guard at each side of Cyclops' throne, which is UC. *There are fires on either side of the throne. Cyclops is seated on the throne*

The demons dance and cavort then crouch on the floor L

Wanda (*struggling with her bonds*) This is crazy! I will never marry you! Let us go!
Cyclops (*his one eye swivelling to look at Wanda*) You will stay until you do as I ask. Will you marry me, Wanda?
Wanda (*trying to stamp her foot*) No-no-no-no-NO!!
Cyclops Once again. Will you marry me?
Wanda Watch my lips. (*She mouths distinctly*) No. No. No.
Cyclops I *am* going to marry you, Wanda.
Wanda (*defiantly*) What part of "NO" don't you understand?
Gryphon You leave her alone, you b-big ugly brute! (*To the audience*) He's just a b-big bully, isn't he, kids!?

They answer "yes"

Cyclops You had better warn your furry friend to be a little more respectful, Wanda, or it will be the worse for both of you. You should be honoured that I wish to marry *you*—a mere mortal!
Wanda (*hotly*) I may be mortal but I'm not *mere*!
Cyclops (*looking at Wanda again*) So what's your problem, Wanda? I'm rich, powerful, famous... Isn't that all you ever wanted?
Wanda It used to be all I wanted. (*She considers*) But now I know that when I marry, I want to be ... in love.
Cyclops (*roaring*) LOVE!? LOVE!? (*He laughs*) What would you know about love? You've never loved anybody except yourself! (*Menacingly*)

Act II, Scene 6   45

Say "Yes" to me, Wanda, or I will make things very unpleasant for you. Do I have to turn up the heat a little to convince you? (*He gestures to the demons*)

The demons start stoking up the fires on either side of the throne. As the song progresses, Wanda and Gingernut show increasing discomfort as the temperature rises. This song is sung in a cruel, teasing way by the demons as they goad the prisoners

Song 19 (Demons' song and dance)

The demons take up their spears and start poking the prisoners, their threats becoming more and more aggressive until they finish in a circle with their spears almost touching Wanda and the Gryphon. Cyclops laughs throughout all this

One more time, Wanda. Will you marry me? Say "No" once more, and I will have your fine feathered friend plucked and turned into a finger-lickin' gooood snack!

The demons next to Gingernut gleefully start to pluck out his fur and fling pieces in the air. He cries out and flinches. Wanda can bear it no longer

Wanda Stop it! All right, Cyclops! I'll marry you.
Cyclops (*teasing her*) But only if you *love* me, Wanda.

Gingernut is plucked again

Wanda (*watching in horror*) Yes! Yes! I love you!
Cyclops (*jovially, winking his eye with each "ay"*) Ay, ay! That's better. (*To the guards*) Untie her!
Wanda Tell them to stop hurting Gingernut!
Cyclops (*to the guards*) Leave him alone!

The guards back off the Gryphon reluctantly. They untie both from their poles

So you promise you will marry me, Wanda? Of your own free will?
Wanda I promise.
Cyclops And you will love me?
Wanda Yes.
Cyclops Then say it.
Wanda I... I promise to love you, Cyclops. (*She sighs*) And I will marry you.
Cyclops YES!! YES!! (*He roars with laughter*)

A demon places a veil on Wanda's bowed head. She walks slowly up the centre to Cyclops with Gingernut a pace behind her, as pageboy

Suddenly Hercules swings in on a rope from above

He knocks out a guard with his feet and snatches up his sword

Meanwhile Narcissus runs on from R

An exciting battle ensues. We hear awful sword swishes, thuds, whacks, screams, etc. Gingernut, from a safe place at the side, encourages the audience to cheer our heroes on during the battle. After a sufficiently long battle, Hercules despatches the leader of the Red Guards in a hand to hand fight. Hercules grabs the leader's bow and arrow at the end of the battle

Hercules OK, Cyclops! No more Mr Nice Guy!!

He aims the bow and arrow at Cyclops who is enjoying watching the battle. There is a great roar from the giant. His red eye shuts and his head slumps, he is dead

Scene 7

Frontcloth

Wanda moves DS and falls thankfully into Hercules's arms. Gingernut and Narcissus come forward by their sides

Wanda (*wonderingly*) There *was* someone out there! Hercules!
Hercules (*amazed*) Wanda. Was that *you* singing?
Wanda Was that *you*, Hercules?

They hold each other at arm's length and gaze at each other as if seeing each other properly for the first time

I needed you and you came. Oh, thank you. You saved us, Hercules.

They break apart

And after I've been so awful to everyone! Especially you. How could you risk your life for me?
Hercules I guess that's what the Power of Love can do.

Act II, Scene 7

Wanda (*wonderingly*) The Power of Love...

Song 20 (Reprise of Song 16)—Hercules and Wanda

They move together again during the song. They sing one verse and one chorus, then kiss. Then Wanda turns gently away from him

Oh Hercules! This is all so wonderful. I can't believe it!
Hercules It was meant to happen. The Fates decreed it...
Wanda (*eagerly*) Do you believe in the Fates? So do I.
Hercules Yes, Wanda, I believe in the Fates ... and they believe in you! (*He takes her hands, steps forward, about to hold her again*)

There is the sound of rumbling then crashing

Earthquake! Take cover!

Lighting effects of falling rocks occur during the noise. Wanda screams. Hercules holds her to him protectively, L. Gingernut runs R and crouches in terror, while Narcissus hides behind him

Black-out

Silence

Wanda, are you OK?
Wanda Yes, Hercules. You've saved me again.
Hercules Narcissus?
Narcissus No sweat, Herc. The big guy musta boobytrapped the place!
Wanda Gingernut? Gingernut? Can you hear me? GINGERNUT!

The Lights start to flicker on again

Hercules Hold on, I'm connecting the lights. Don't worry Wanda, we'll soon find your friend.
Wanda (*in horror*) Oh look!

She points to where the Gryphon is lying pinned down. A huge boulder is on his chest. Other rocks are scattered about on the ground. The Lighting returns to normal

Gingernut! GINGERNUT!! (*She rushes to his side and drags frantically at the boulder*) Oh, no!

Narcissus runs forward, tries to budge the rock but fails

He's dead! My only friend! He's dead!

Hercules goes over to the Gryphon, he kneels beside him

Hercules   I think he's still breathing, Wanda. Stand back. (*He lifts the boulder, walks with it and throws it into the wings*)

There is a huge far-off thud of the falling boulder

Wanda   Hercules, that was magnificent! (*She puts her head against Gingernut's chest*) Oh, don't die, Gingernut. Please don't die!

Song 21 (Wanda)

At the end of the song Wanda lays her head on Gingernut

Black-out

They exit

Scene 8

The Palace

The King is seated on his zebra skin throne. He has a thickshake in one hand and is devouring a huge hamburger

Medusa kneels at his feet

Medusa   (*drawing in her breath with a hiss*) Oooh, I adore you when you eat, you big cuddly-wuddly Burger King you!
King   (*he smiles fondly at her, as he eats and drinks*) Hey, baby. (*He holds out the drink*) Care to join me in a thickshake?
Medusa   (*flapping her lashes*) Do you think there'll be room for the both of us?

They giggle together. Then the King whispers something in Medusa's ear. She smirks

   (*Drawing herself up and using a measured tone to resemble Margaret Thatcher*) Kingsy says I look like Margaret Thatcher.

Act II, Scene 8

King Yessir. (*Reverently*) I consider her a National Icon!
Narcissus (*aside, indicating Medusa*) I consider *her* a National eye*sore*!!
Medusa (*whacking him over the head with her purse*) Look, you watch it, you! I've had enough of your lip! The King and I are like *that*! (*She holds up her hand with two fingers closely entwined and uses a sickening baby voice*) Aren't we, Kingsy-Wingsy!?

King stands, takes her in his arms—which isn't easy, and chucks her under the chin

King Yeah, ma cute lil chocolate cupcake...!
Medusa (*pinching his cheek*) My hunky double beefburger!
King (*getting amorous*) Gimme a kiss, Sugarlips!
Medusa (*getting coy*) Ooooh, stop it! Stop it!
King (*all over her*) C'mon, pucker up...!
Medusa (*fighting him off, less and less firmly*) Don't! Stop it! ... Don't! ... Stop! ... Don't! Stop! Don't stop!

The King nuzzles her neck and whispers something in her ear. Medusa squeals then biffs him in the tummy with her handbag

Oooooooooh, you saucy old King, you!

He staggers backward and falls to the floor

Narcissus (*curiously*) What did he say, Auntie?
Medusa (*briskly*) You're too young to know. (*She looks at her watch, then listens to it*) But I'll tell you this; even my shock-proof watch was embarrassed!!
King (*shuffling over on his knees*) Medusa, baby! You're the gal for me! May ah have your hand in marriage?
Medusa (*pulling him to her by the ear; affecting a Southern drawl*) Kingsy-pie, you can have *any* lil ole part of me you want!
King (*they embrace*) Pussycat!
Medusa Teddybear!

Song 22 (The King) (backed by the Chorus)

The Chorus enters L

They perform as a backing group as the King moves forward to the microphone to sing to Medusa. During the song, which she is thrilled about, she tries the throne for size and likes it. At the end of the number they fling themselves madly into each other's arms again

Narcissus makes a finger down throat motion to the audience and leaves US, shaking his head in disbelief

Come on, my great big cuddly-wuddly Teddybear. Let's make hay while the iron's hot! We must see about a marriage licence!

Medusa and the King skip out hand-in-hand, L

The "Hercules" chant begins

The Cheerleaders enter US *with pompoms and form an aisle from* US *to* DS

Wanda enters with Hercules at her side, smiling proudly. They come forward down the aisle

Hercules (*looking at her lovingly*) Today I have married the most beautiful girl in the world. My Wanda-Woman!
Wanda Oh, Hercules. You've changed me into a completely new person.
Hercules (*very fondly*) No, Wanda. *You've* done that all by yourself.
Wanda Not by myself. Remember my Friend, Gingernut. *He* was the one who taught me how important love is. If only we could've saved him.

We hear someone off L *calling "Wanda! Wanda!" Everyone looks up from their sad contemplation*

Suddenly Gingernut flies in L, *complete with wonderful full-sized wings! (See Production Notes)*

Gryphon Whew! I made it! The sky's j-j-jolly high up there, you know. (*He waves to Wanda*) Hi, Wanda! (*He waves to the audience*) Hullo, everyone!

He elicits the reply "Hullo, Gingernut"

Wanda (*watching delightedly as he lands*) GINGERNUT!! You're alive! You can fly! (*She rushes to him and hugs him*)
Gryphon Careful of the wings! They've only just grown.
Wanda (*stepping back and walking around him to look at them*) Oh, they're wonderful! You're wonderful! What happened?
Hercules (*coming over too*) I don't believe it! Gingernut, we thought you were dead. (*He thinks again*) You *were* dead!
Gryphon Yes, but the Fates gave me another spin of the Wheel. I kept my promise that I'd be your friend, Wanda, and now I can fly!
Wanda That's great, Gingernut. But will you still want to be my friend now?

Act II, Scene 8

Gryphon Of course, silly! I'll always be your friend. (*To the audience*) Friends are forever, aren't they, kids!?

He elicits a "yes" response

Wanda (*hugging him*) Oh, Gingernut, I'm so happy! We've got marvellous news too. Hercules and I have just got married!

Medusa enters, on the King's arm, from L

Medusa (*to the others*) And I'm marrying the King!
King (*sickeningly*) Baby-love!
Medusa (*dotingly*) Punnykins!
King If we're gonna tie the knot, Medoosy-woosy, ah'd sure like to see what ah'm gettin'. Gimme just a lil peep under that hat, will ya, honey?
Medusa (*to the audience*) Oh dear. Should I?

She elicits a response, decides to take it off anyway and does so. Then she looks at the King in horror. He is standing frozen—like a statue

(*Beating her breast in despair*) Oh, curses! He's stoned! Just before we've signed the marriage licence! Just before I've dotted me t's and crossed me i's!! (*She swoons, very OTT, and slides down the front of the King's body to the floor*)

Narcissus enters

Narcissus Zeus! Auntie's fainted clean away! (*He kneels beside her, holding up her head gingerly*)

Chloë and Zoë run on

Chloë ⎫ (*together; seeing Medusa*) Oh no!
Zoë ⎭
Narcissus (*calling off* R) Herc! Herc! Can you bring us a pillow?
Hercules (*sounding somewhat surprised*) What? Oh, OK.

Hercules and Wanda exit

The King unfreezes during this and chuckles as Medusa sits up

King Hey, Doosie-Woosie! I was only foolin'! (*He helps her up*) Come on, let's be havin' that weddin'!

Medusa (*flinging her arms around the King's neck*) Ooooh, you naughty boy! Kingsy, you're a one!

Hercules enters R, *followed by Wanda. He is carrying an enormous pillar held in both arms high above his head like a weightlifter*

Hercules Well, here's the pillar. (*He looks round*) Where do you want me to put it?

Medusa (*looking at the King, smiling her wicked smile*) Don't tempt me! (*They embrace*)

Hercules grins and stands the pillar up at at the side

Wanda Hercules—you're a legend!!

And they embrace too, while Narcissus puts a very friendly arm around Chloë and Zoë

Song 23 (Hercules and Cast)

CURTAIN

PRODUCTION NOTES

Costume Suggestions

ACT I

Scene 1

The Greek Chorus wear white sheets draped into a toga style and pinned at the shoulder.

The eight Cheerleaders should look very cute in short skirts and tight T-shirts each with a letter of Hercules' name emblazoned on it. Every time they line up they will thus spell out their hero's name (except when required to spell out other words as given in the script). It is most effective if they are dressed in two strong colours to imply they are Hercules' team. They each carry two big cheerleader pompoms.

Scene 2

Venus must have a powerful, sensuous aura. She wears a long white Grecian-styled gown that can flow from her shoulders and from below the bust to actually become the mountain itself. (See Production Notes regarding Venus' Mountain.) She is composed of two women—the second woman standing on the platform right behind Venus is concealed by a long veil flowing from Venus' starburst head-dress. Their four arms wave in exotic motions and point or gesticulate as Venus speaks. Her microphone can change from hand to hand to hand to hand as she sings!

The Nymphs wear filmy flowing tunics in sky colours—blues, mauves, etc., which swirl sensuously as they dance around the base of Venus' mountain.

The Gryphon is a tubby little mythical beast with a cuddly-looking lion's body covered in ginger-coloured fur. There must be one portion of his "coat" that has some pieces of fur attached with Velcro so that they can be ripped off dramatically by the Demons in Act II. His mask will be quite light and stable if it is built using a cycling helmet as a base. This can then be fastened under the chin. Feathers and a smiling curved beak can be built up using papier mâché, and shiny silver-button eyes can then be added. Spraying with metallic bronze paint will strengthen the mask and add a realistic sheen. The Gryphon has a tiny pair of ineffectual wings (which can also be sprayed with this paint) on his back.

Scene 3

Wanda should look beautiful in a long elegant gown and dainty sandals. Chloë and Zoë are dressed in simple long shifts, with circlets around their heads.

Scene 4

The YMCA male chorus can wear present-day gym gear e.g. lycra shorts, muscle shirts, etc. They may wear sneakers or sandals thonged up the legs with tape.

If he has a great physique, Hercules can wear an open-chested short tunic . Otherwise he can look equally effective in long-sleeved tunic and trousers that have been suitably padded for a muscular effect. They should be in the same "team" colours as worn by his cheerleaders.

Some fun can be had with Narcissus' clothes e.g. sneakers and turned-backwards cap American-style, teamed with a short funky tunic.

Scene 5

The Three Fates are outrageously colourful. They could each wear a long gown slit up the side and high heels. Bold colours that clash, e.g. scarlet, orange and purple satin would be effective for the three gowns. The Three Fates should have marvellous piled-up hairdos and startling jewellery and make-up.

Scene 6

Medusa strives for a fashionable look. She is busty, wearing a long, gaudy floral gown. This is Grecian style but slit almost to the waist one side to reveal high heels (with crisscrossed laces up hairy male legs if the part is played by a male). Loud frilly bloomers may be glimpsed. She wears a colour co-ordinated turban which can be unwound or removed easily. Under this is the snake wig which forms Medusa's hair. This can be made from a flesh-coloured bathing cap of the old-fashioned snug-fitting kind. Many small rubbery toy snakes are sewn onto or wired into this by the tails. Some can be wired onto springs to give a bouncing effect when moved.

Production Notes   55

Scene 7

The Red Guards wear red Roman-style tunics or T-shirts and shorts under red Roman armour. Strong cardboard, painted red and cut into strips then joined with strong adhesive tape (leaving gaps to allow articulation so the Guards can move easily), works well. Epaulettes for the breastplates can be cardboard with red vinyl strips hanging from the edge. Each breastplate has a single huge black and white eye painted on it, front and back, most looking straight ahead but one or two can look to the side. Some fun can be had by positioning the Red Guards side by side so that two eyes seem to squint in towards each other. The kilts can be made of red vinyl cut into strips and attached to a waistband. Sandals, thonged up the legs, if desired, complete the uniform—Roman helmets are optional.

Scene 8

The Bodyguards are in black, top to toe. They wear present-day T-shirts, long trousers, black shoes and socks and black wrap-around sunshades.

The King is squeezed into a gorgeous white satin jumpsuit with a high turned-up collar. It is encrusted with rhinestones. He may also wear a short purple cape and white boots. He has a wide belt with an awesome buckle and wears several huge rings. His black hair is in a pompadour style. One or two little towels are around his neck.

The Greek Chorus can brighten up the stage in swirly rock'n'roll skirts and tops in bright colours. They may wear bobby socks and black pumps, and perhaps a small bright neckerchief. Some ponytail hairdos would add to the effect too.

Medusa has put on her best turban and a mangey-looking fur stole, possibly fox.

ACT II

Scene 1

Medusa wears a crossover-front pinny or housecoat over her gown, and she has on a pair of pink rubber gloves. On her head she wears a scarf tied at the front with a knot, Mrs Mop style. She is wearing striped rugby socks, a strident pair of frilly bloomers and is on roller-blades. Possibly she has elbow and knee protectors on as well. Depending on how far she is going to strip, she can wear several layers of awful petticoats.

Narcissus is now in very tight black trousers and a black or emerald green satin shirt with full, ballet-style sleeves. He has black dancing shoes.

The Slaves are wearing black leotards, black tights and short full skirts in black or emerald green (to co-ordinate with Narcissus). Their black shoes are suitable for Irish dancing.

Scene 3

The Greek Chorus have changed their sheets! They now wear floral, striped or plain coloured sheets—one could wear a white sheet with "Property of (local) Hospital" boldly stencilled down its side!

Narcissus has quickly added an army camouflage jacket and helmet to his attire.

Scene 6

The Demons (male and/or female dancers, or children) should be clad in "hot"-coloured full-length bodysuits or leotards and tights. Red, orange, yellow, hot pink and black are all suitable. They can wear small horned masks and carry tridents or spears if desired.

For Cyclops see Scenery Production Notes.

Scene 8

The King might wish to wear something even more flashy than before (literally!) in the form of a jumpsuit with many tiny coloured flashing lights decorating the collar, chest, etc.

Medusa is resplendent in a new full-length gown for the wedding, possibly sequined. The bust is very pronounced, being two gold cones à la Madonna, and a black tassel hangs from the centre of each. These (with a flick of the torso and a little practice) can be twirled in time to the music!

The Greek Chorus are in their rock'n'roll outfits again.

Wanda looks amazing in her wedding outfit. She can wear a Wonder Woman type bodice outfit in white and silver (or gold). From each side of her wide silver belt flows diaphanous white material forming a cutaway skirt that reveals her legs. She wears lycra tights and a pair of long white or silver boots to continue the Wonder Woman effect. On her head is a silver coronet from which a long filmy white veil flows down her back.

Production Notes

Hercules should be dressed in the same colours as Wanda (white and silver or gold) to look especially handsome. He has a laurel leaf wreath of silver or gold on his head.

Chloë and Zoë will be dressed more elaborately than usual for the occasion, perhaps as matching Grecian bridesmaids.

Narcissus can again wear his ACT II, Scene 1 dancing outfit if desired, or a flash new outfit.

Gryphon now has a beautiful full-size pair of wings, the same colour as his previous ones.

Suggested Scenery And Special Props

ACT I

NB: Throughout *Hercules—The Panto!!* every attempt has been made to keep the pace going without long pauses. There is no need at any stage for a black-out in which to change scenes because the Greek Chorus make any quick changes, wheeling on the various trucks etc. as an integral part of the action itself. Large items such as Venus' mountain and Cyclops' throne are built on trucks which will be positioned behind tabs during the preceding scene.

Scene 2

Maximum dramatic effect is sought when the curtains open on this scene. Purple lighting, dry ice, flashes of lightning, etc. can increase the drama. Venus' mountain can be based on a high inverted-cone-shaped scaffold constructed of wood. This should be firmly built onto a truck and have a ladder up the back and a small platform at the top large enough for the two women who make up Venus to stand one in front of the other. A frame for them to lean forward and back against will increase the safety factor. The mountain should be as high as possible taking into consideration the height of Venus herself, height of the stage and sightlines, lighting, etc. The body of the mountain is covered with white material from the summit to the foot, giving the impression of snow. Venus' gown will be of the same material so the mountain seems to be a continuation of her gown, flowing from an empire line below the bust to the hem. Venus is only seen from above the waist at any time.

Scene 3

Here are some suggestions for the placards carried by the Greek Chorus in their protest march: A placard reading "Why should men wear the pants?" can be followed by one another reading "Down with them all!" "A woman needs a man like a fish needs a bicycle". "Girlpower!" "No men? Amen!" "We support the Trojan Women". The final placard shown when the song mentions "the President" could have a caricature of President Clinton and the words "Silly Billy".

Scene 5

The Three Fates' knitting is very important to the plot. Knit is working on "Princess Wanda"—a short, ugly piece of knitting in muddy greens, browns or greys. It should be in a very plain coarse pattern such as garter stitch and have no redeeming features whatsoever. Purl has a gorgeous piece of knitting: "Liz Taylor". It is flamboyantly patterned in gold, purple, shocking pink, emerald, scarlet—whatever will look vibrant and exciting. An interesting mix of patterns e.g. blackberry stitch, zigzags, etc. means it has no dull patches, but every now and then there should be a touch of the "blues"! This "Life" should be *very* long, and rolled up at first so it can be dramatically unrolled towards the audience when Purl shows it off. Drop One is struggling with a medium-length piece in black or navy with fine white stripes which should resemble business suit fabric. However the pinstripes veer off-course quite badly and quite often. Also the entire piece features several large holes from dropped stitches which Drop One pokes her fingers through occasionally.

On the Three Fates' truck is a Wheel of Fortune on a tall stand, such as those used at fairgrounds for winning instant prizes. A fancy cover thrown over the Wheel hides the lettering which can later be revealed to show knitting instructions written around the Wheel where the numbers would normally be. Examples: "Change to pink" "In the red" "Keep it plain" "Repeat the last ten years in grey" "Watch the tension!" "Introduce some blues" and "Cast Off!". The Wheel is rigged in such a way that, when spun, it will always stop with the arrow pointing to "Cast Off!"

This scene can be made very appealing to children by the addition of a puppet show. Before Song 5, two Greek Chorus members carry on a large curtain which hangs from a rod. This can be held up in front of the Fates to hide them as they perform with their hand puppets (made from pink knitted socks) moving along the top of the curtain. If the song *Que Sera Sera* is used, suitable puppets would be a "mother" (white cotton wool hair and round glasses on the sock puppet) operated by Knit, seated stage right, a "girl" (fluffy yellow wool hair with a big bow in it) operated by Purl in the centre and the "boy" (black wool hair and a moustache which can be stuck on or taken off quickly as needed) for Drop One on stage left. They can sing in suitable funny childlike voices etc. as the lines of the song dictate, and the "girl" can exchange her bow for a wedding veil at the appropriate verse. All will join in the choruses. The "boy" can double as "husband" (with moustache added) as well as being the "child" again at the end of the song. They wave, calling "Goodbye" to the audience as they are wheeled off at the end of the number.

Scene 6

A standing street sign outside the rear doors of the salon, in the street, reads "Easy St". The salon interior should be ultra feminine—everything decked out in lolly pink and silver to suit Medusa's taste. A sign over the doorway proclaims, "The Royal Heir Beauty Salon—For Your Crowning Glory". Under this is written "Phone xxxivvxii" or similar nonsense Roman numerals. There should be a vanity cabinet with a large mirror above it on either side of the stage to give the impression of hair-washing facilities etc. These can hold hand mirrors, brushes, vases of pink flowers, etc. At least one free-standing old fashioned hair-drier that can be rolled around is required, plus two hairdressing chairs on wheels and two wheeled hairdressing trays on stands which contain curlers and various props as needed.

Medusa should take the soprano line of any song performed here. If the song *Anything You Can Do I Can Do Better* is used, here are some suggestions for business and funny props to increase the fun. When Narcissus sings the line "I can live on bread and cheese" he gets a large loaf of bread and a chunk of cheese from the props tray which has been wheeled over, and holds them up. He will be about to take a bite of the loaf when Medusa pulls a large "dead rat" out of it by the tail and holds it up, singing the line "So can a rat!" Narcissus hurriedly throws the loaf and cheese into the wings in disgust. When Medusa sings "Yes I can!" (...sing higher) she can make a great show of climbing on the hairdressing chair to reach the very high notes in falsetto. For the "I can buy anything cheaper than you" lines Narcissus bangs a funny gag plastic gavel that squeaks, as if they are at an auction, as they call "Fifty pence, forty pence" etc., ending with Medusa snatching it from him to bop him on the head. On the line "I can say anything softer than you" Medusa will produce a conchshell hearing-trumpet which she will put to her ear to hear Narcissus when he sings very quietly. But the last time he sings "Yes I can" he will actually bellow this directly into the trumpet so that Medusa jumps into the air with shock. On Narcissus' line "I can open any safe" he will hold up a round black "bomb" with a wick to which a fluoro "flame" is attached. It has the word "Bomb" clearly lettered on it in white. He will throw it to Medusa who will frantically throw it back to him.

The band then plays till ready while Narcissus and Medusa milk the scene. They will both go on tossing the bomb backwards and forwards several more times, juggling it from hand to hand as they race around panic-stricken, looking for a safe place to dump it. Medusa, during an anticipatory drum roll from the band, can pretend she is going to toss the bomb to a child in the audience but instead throws it to the band leader. He tosses it back to her in horror. Finally Narcissus receives it and hurls it into the wings. They cover their ears and cower. Silence. Then "Boooooom"! The number then continues to the end.

Scene 8

If the Red Guards are doubling up as the Bodyguards in the next scene they will need to exit smartly for a quick change straight after Song 8. If not, they can remain onstage during the dialogue and reprise the song at the end of the scene if desired.

Scene 9

The palace should be a monument to bad taste. The pillars on either side of the staircase can be painted in jungle patterns e.g. a pair in black and white zebra stripes, a pair with leopard spots or tiger stripes etc. If there are windows they should be very tall and graced with animal print drapes with swags and tails (maybe tigertails!). There can be a shrine effect if desired, featuring a portrait of a very grim-faced woman to which the King can refer lovingly when he mentions his "Momma". Maybe there could be a big stuffed red-satin-heart cushion on the throne with "Momma" worked on it in florid script.

ACT II

Scene 1

The props must be carefully checked and in place before this scene opens, for the suggested business to work smoothly. For the "Beatles haircut" gag, a suitably styled dark wig, with a few large toy "beetles" entwined in it, is inserted hair-downwards in a deep round basin beforehand. Care must be taken to keep the wig positioned properly on the boy's head whilst removing the basin. This is most effective if the boy has dark hair similar to the wig in colour but not in style. For the girl's hair-colouring gag, an outrageous punk wig, green or perhaps multi-coloured, is taped hair-upwards inside the hair-drier. The hair-drier must be placed onstage and moved in such a way that the audience cannot look up into it and see the wig. The wig is then positioned

Production Notes 61

on the girl's head by the Slaves as the drier is moved carefully away to reveal the new hairstyle. This can easily be done while the Slaves stand around the drier blocking the view. The showdown at the end of the scene should include lots of action, spraying and shouting. Narcissus can hand the girl a spray pump full of water (marked "Setting Lotion") and tell her to spray Medusa and Medusa can do the same with the boy. If spray cans are used they should contain plastic "fun spaghetti" or something similar, but be marked "Hairspray". Cans containing whipped cream are marked "Shaving Cream". Any make-up, wigs, etc. are removed and the children return to the audience.

Scene 2

This scene may be deleted but it serves as a safety measure if the stage is wet or messy, and gives Narcissus more time to clean himself up (if necessary) and perhaps add an army jacket and helmet before entering again through the audience.

Scene 3

Hercules can wear a bow strapped to his back and a quiver of arrows, or the bow and an arrow can be snatched from the Leader of the Red Guards later during the battle action. The latter would be an easier option for Hercules as he would then be unhindered by the bow during this and following scenes.

The boat needs to be one-sided only and have a seat or two inside. It can be pushed across the stage readily if on wheels which are hidden by painted waves beneath the boat.

Scene 5

Knit's knitting has changed for the better. Another piece of knitting identical to the first is used, but added to the latest part of it is a pretty, interestingly-patterned portion perhaps in rich yellow and red. Though there is only a little of it, it's a very obvious improvement.

Scene 6

Cyclops' grotto should be awesome, even topping Venus' mountain for dramatic statement. This is a full stage scene, the throne being set behind tabs during the previous scene. A frieze of stalagmites can encircle the stage and stalactites can hang from above. All will be bathed in red light which can change to oranges, yellows, etc., if desired, especially during the song. Dry ice which has been produced before the curtain opens completes the hot subterranean effect required here. A good effect can be achieved if "jets of flame" shoot up before the song. These come from two small stalagmite cones hard against the sides of the throne each containing an electric fan pointing upwards. The wiring is concealed beside the throne. Red plastic "flames" tied to the fan grill will shoot up and continue to flicker as soon as the fans are switched on.

As for Cyclops himself, he is seated on an enormous throne which seems to have been crafted out of the stalagmites themselves. It can be built in wood on a truck and covered with canvas or similar, draped and painted in "hot" colours to give a natural, rocky effect. Cyclops should be as big as possible. The operator will stand on the seat of the throne and thus be inside the giant's torso. Huge mock legs jut out from the torso towards the audience, bend at the knee and end down at the floor in a pair of large bare feet, as if he is seated. The torso, arms and thighs can be padded on a framework of hosing or wire, and large cardboard cylinders cut in half make very effective shoulders, legs, etc. A drapery of white material stapled over the torso and legs gives the effect of a toga, and this can also cover the arms like long sleeves. Thus only the hands, feet and head are actually seen. These can be made of pink foam, the hands can appear to clutch the armrests of the throne if they are wired within and the fingers bent into a natural shape. The head is constructed from pink sheets of foam over a wire frame and painted with a fearsome sneer. A white beard and hair made from mop-string look impressively shaggy. His one big eye, in the centre of his forehead, can use a working red light or reflector tape. The operator, arms held up inside the giant's hollow head, can move the eye to each side to watch the action, and blink a shutter-type lid occasionally. At the death-blow he will slam the eyelid shut and slump the head forward. For a more ambitious Cyclops the operator can shake the chest while the giant laughs and even use one arm to point. Cyclops can even appear about to rise out of his throne at the end, if sufficient leverage is installed inside and he contains a well-rehearsed operator or two.

The battle scene should be full of noisy action. Strobes or cycling lights may be used to create excitement. Hercules must equip himself with a sword snatched from a Red Guard and perhaps commandeer another and throw it to Narcissus. Effects include awful war cries, screams, yells and sword swishes and clangs. As many witty stunts as possible, e.g. somersaults, sword juggling, cartwheels, etc. can be incorporated, e.g. when two Red Guards are attacking Hercules, one from either side, he can step back at the last minute and smack their heads together. Hercules could attack the two guards who stand either side of Cyclops' throne. He fights them behind the throne then tosses out their lifeless bodies—a floppy full-size dummy dressed as a Red Guard comes flying out from each side. Narcissus can swing a big sword

Production Notes   63

round in a circle so the Guards have to jump as it approaches their feet. Hercules could let him fight piggy-back ... the ideas are endless.

Scene 8

This can be another room in the palace or simply have a throne added.

The flying Gryphon does not need to involve the real actor and a costly harness, although these would be the ideal. This scene can be very successful if a dummy Gryphon with large wings is flown across the back of the stage on a wire, in a flying Superman pose, arms outstretched before him! He must be released from a height in the wings UL and come swooping across and down into the wings exiting UR. This is accompanied by Gryphon's voice calling to Wanda and then a thump and the sound of running feet before the real Gryphon comes panting on DR.

The pillar brought on by Hercules should look like the other pillars throughout the King's palace. Naturally it is made of light polystyrene but Hercules will carry it so it looks like the real thing! It will need a base so he can stand it upright to one side.

Song 22. Hercules can sing the first verse to Wanda, then the remainder of the song is ideal for walkdowns and audience singalong in the repeated choruses. A suitable order for walkdowns would be: Bodyguards, Cheerleaders (then Red Guards, Nymphs, Demons if they are not the same actors), Greek Chorus, Zoë and Chloë, Venus, The Three Fates, Gryphon, The King, Medusa, Narcissus, Wanda and Hercules.

FURNITURE AND PROPERTY LIST

See Production Notes for details and further suggestions

ACT I

SCENE 1

Personal: **Cheerleaders:** pompoms (carried throughout)

SCENE 2

On stage: **Venus'** mountain. *In it*: large volume with bold title "This is Your Wife"

Personal: **Venus:** watch (worn throughout)

SCENE 3

Off stage: Small table holding glass of wine, packet of gingernut biscuits, archaic conchshell "telephone", plate of fruit (**Chloë**)
Chaise longue with **Wanda** (**Chorus**)
Portable TV set, potato peeler (**Zoë**)
Remote control (**Princess**)
Placards with funny feminist slogans (**Zoë**, **Chloë**, and **Chorus**)

SCENE 4

On stage: YMCA sign

SCENE 5

Off stage: **Three Fates** truck with three barstools, "Wheel of Fortune" lottery wheel, varieties of knitting (**Demi-chorus**)

Personal: **Demi-chorus:** watches

Furniture and Property List   65

SCENE 6

On stage: "Easy St." sign
              "The Royal Heir Beauty Salon" sign
              Vanity cabinets
              Trayful of props
              Mirrors
              Conchshell bowl
              2 hand-mirrors
              Shampoo
              Chair

Off stage: Salon armchair with **Wanda**, pedicure things, biscuits, grapes (**Zoë** and **Chloë**)
              Scroll with sign of big, red eye on back (**Zoë**)

Personal: **Wanda**: bright blue "mudpack" mask, slices of cucumber, curlers, big pink hairdressing bib

SCENE 7

Off stage: Spears (**Guards**)

Personal: **Wanda**: manacles attached to chain
              Gryphon: manacles attached to chain

SCENE 8

On stage: Microphone on stand
              Momma's shrine

Personal: **King**: huge rings, towels

ACT II

SCENE 1

On stage: Salon props as Act I, Scene 6
              "Beatles" wig in deep basin
              Feather duster
              Air freshener
              Outsize stuffed or polystyrene "hand"
              Urn

Poster of someone with shaven head
Poster of a punk
Make-up
Spray bottles and cans
Aerosol of whipped cream
Razor

Off stage: Broom (**Medusa**)
2 chairs (**Slaves**)
Huge pair of scissors, old-fashioned hair-drier on wheeled stand.
In it: punk wig (**Slaves**)

Personal: **Medusa**: tiny battery-driven propellor fan, shoes, pink rubber gloves, huge magnifying glass

SCENE 2

Off stage: Mop and bucket (**Medusa**)

SCENE 3

Off stage: Street map (**Narcissus**)
Signs on stands; "River Styx" and "The Other Side" (**Chorus**)
Small boat mounted on truck (**Chorus**)
Three Fates truck (**Demi-chorus**)

SCENE 4

On stage: **Venus'** mountain as Act I, Scene 2

SCENE 5

On stage: Large rock

Off stage: **Three Fates** truck (**Demi-chorus**)

SCENE 6

On stage: Two upright poles
Cyclops' throne
"Fires" on either side of the throne
Spears
Veil
Bows and arrows

Furniture and Property List

SCENE 7

Off stage: Huge boulder (**ASM**)

SCENE 8

On stage: **King**'s throne
Thickshake
Huge hamburger
Medusa's handbag
Microphone

Off stage: Enormous pillar (**Hercules**)

Personal: **Medusa:** purse

LIGHTING PLOT

Property fittings required: nil
Various interior and exterior settings

ACT I, SCENE 1

To open: Overall general lighting

No cues

ACT I, SCENE 2

To open: Dramatic lightning, purple spot on **Venus**

No cues

ACT I, SCENE 3

To open: Overall general lighting

Cue 1   **Zoë** wheels on TV set   (Page 5)
          TV lighting effect from TV set

Cue 2   **Zoë** and **Chloë** clear table and TV   (Page 8)
          Cut TV lighting effect

ACT I, SCENE 4

To open: Overall general lighting

No cues

ACT I, SCENE 5

To open: Overall general lighting

No cues

Lighting Plot

ACT I, SCENE 6

To open: Overall general lighting

No cues

ACT I, SCENE 7

To open: Overall general lighting

No cues

ACT I, SCENE 8

To open: Overall general lighting

No cues

ACT II, SCENE 1

To open: Overall general lighting

No cues

ACT II, SCENE 2

To open: Overall general lighting

No cues

ACT II, SCENE 3

To open: Watery lighting representing River Styx

No cues

ACT II, SCENE 4

To open: Overall general lighting

No cues

ACT II, Scene 5

To open: Overall general lighting

No cues

ACT II, Scene 6

To open: Spooky lighting

No cues

ACT II, Scene 7

To open: Overall general lighting

Cue 3	**Hercules**: "Earthquake! Take cover!" *Lighting effects of falling rocks*	(Page 47)
Cue 4	**Narcissus** hides near the throne *Black-out*	(Page 47)
Cue 5	**Wanda**: "GINGERNUT!" *Flicker lights on*	(Page 47)
Cue 6	**Wanda** points to **Gryphon** *Bring up lights to normal*	(Page 47)
Cue 7	**Wanda** lays her head on **Gingernut** *Black-out*	(Page 48)

ACT II, Scene 8

To open: Overall general lighting

No cues

EFFECTS PLOT

ACT I

Cue 1	To open Scene 2 *Very dramatic crack of thunder, dry ice effect*	(Page 2)
Cue 2	**Chorus** exit *Final strains of a TV theme*	(Page 5)
Cue 3	**Chorus** exit *End music*	(Page 5)
Cue 4	**Wanda**: "Don't say I'm not good to you…" *Phone rings, tolling like a handbell*	(Page 6)
Cue 5	**King** sings, gyrates, throws towel to audience *Screaming fans, repeated at end of song*	(Page 26)
Cue 6	Audience echoes "Long live the King!" *Sound of man screaming as if being murdered*	(Page 26)
Cue 7	**Voice From Box**: "Sorry. How's this?" *Fans screaming*	(Page 26)

ACT II

Cue 8	To open Scene 6 *Smoky, subterranean effects*	(Page 44)
Cue 9	Battle starts *Awful battle sounds of sword swishes, thuds, whacks, screams*	(Page 46)
Cue 10	**Hercules** takes **Wanda**'s hands, steps forward *Sound of rumbling then crashing*	(Page 47)

Cue 11	Black-out *Silence*	(Page 47)
Cue 12	**Hercules** throws boulder off *Huge far-off thud of falling boulder*	(Page 48)